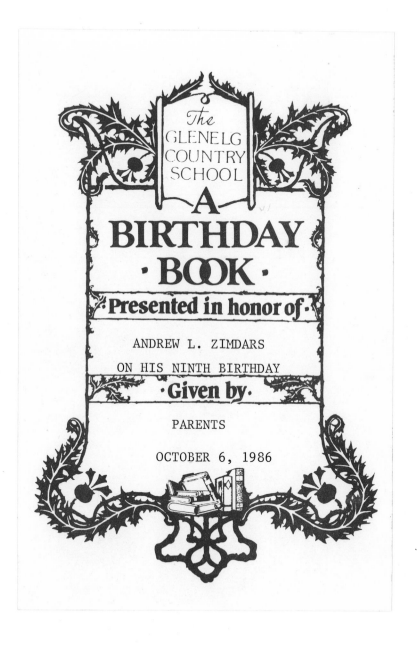

The
GLENELG
COUNTRY
SCHOOL

A
BIRTHDAY
· BOOK ·

· Presented in honor of ·

ANDREW L. ZIMDARS

ON HIS NINTH BIRTHDAY

· Given by ·

PARENTS

OCTOBER 6, 1986

ANDREW JACKSON

ANDREW JACKSON

Herman J. Viola

1986
CHELSEA HOUSE PUBLISHERS
NEW YORK
NEW HAVEN   PHILADELPHIA

SENIOR EDITOR: William P. Hansen
ASSOCIATE EDITORS: Jane Crain
                   John Haney
                   Marian W. Taylor
EDITORIAL COORDINATOR: Karyn Gullen Browne
EDITORIAL STAFF: Pierre Hauser
                 Perry Scott King
                 Kathleen McDermott
                 Howard Ratner
                 Alma Rodriguez-Sokol
                 John Selfridge
ART DIRECTOR: Susan Lusk
LAYOUT: Irene Friedman
ART ASSISTANTS: Noreen Lamb
               Victoria Tomaselli
COVER DESIGN: Carol McDougall
PICTURE RESEARCH: Ian Ensign

First Printing

Library of Congress Cataloging in Publication Data

Viola, Herman J. ANDREW JACKSON

(World leaders past & present)
Bibliography: p.
Includes index
   [1. Jackson, Andrew, 1767–1845—Juvenile literature.
2. Presidents—United States—Biography—Juvenile
literature.   [1. Jackson, Andrew, 1767–1845.
2. Presidents]   I. Title.   II. Series.
E382.V56   1986   973.5'6'0924 [B] [92]   86-2237
ISBN 0-87754-587-1

Chelsea House Publishers
Harold Steinberg, Chairman and Publisher
Susan Lusk, Vice President
A Division of Chelsea House Educational Communications, Inc.

133 Christopher Street, New York, NY 10014

345 Whitney Avenue, New Haven, CT 06510

5014 West Chester Pike, Edgemont, PA 19028

Photos courtesy of Art Resource, The Bettmann Archive, Library of Congress, The National Archives, The New-York Historical Society, The Smithsonian Institution, and the Woolaroc Museum (Bartlesville, Oklahoma)

Contents

CHELSEA HOUSE PUBLISHERS

WORLD LEADERS PAST & PRESENT

Further titles in preparation

ON LEADERSHIP
Arthur M. Schlesinger, jr.

LEADERSHIP, it may be said, is really what makes the world go round. Love no doubt smooths the passage; but love is a private transaction between consenting adults. Leadership is a public transaction with history. The idea of leadership affirms the capacity of individuals to move, inspire and mobilize masses of people so that they act together in pursuit of an end. Sometimes leadership serves good purposes, sometimes bad; but whether the end is benign or evil, great leaders are those men and women who leave their personal stamp on history.

Now, the very concept of leadership implies the proposition that individuals can make a difference. This proposition has never been universally accepted. From classical times to the present day, eminent thinkers have regarded individuals as no more than the agents and pawns of larger forces, whether the gods and goddesses of the ancient world or, in the modern era, race, class, nation, the dialectic, the will of the people, the spirit of the times, history itself. Against such forces, the individual dwindles into insignificance.

So contends the thesis of historical determinism. Tolstoy's great novel *War and Peace* offers a famous statement of the case. Why, Tolstoy asked, did millions of men in the Napoleonic wars, denying their human feelings and their common sense, move back and forth across Europe slaughtering their fellows? "The war," Tolstoy answered, "was bound to happen simply because it was bound to happen." All prior history predetermined it. As for leaders, they, Tolstoy said, "are but the labels that serve to give a name to an end and, like labels, they have the least possible connection with the event." The greater the leader, "the more conspicuous the inevitability and the predestination of every act he commits." The leader, said Tolstoy, is "the slave of history."

Determinism takes many forms. Marxism is the determinism of class, Nazism the determinism of race. But the idea of men and women as the slaves of history runs athwart the deepest human instincts. Rigid determinism abolishes the idea of human freedom—the assumption of free choice that underlies every move we make, every word we speak, every thought we think. It abolishes the idea of human responsibility, since it is manifestly unfair to reward or punish people for actions that are by definition beyond their control. No one can live consistently by any deterministic creed. The Marxist states prove this themselves by their extreme susceptibility to the cult of leadership.

More than that, history refutes the idea that individuals make no difference. In December 1931 a British politician crossing Park Avenue in New York City between 76th and 77th Streets around ten-thirty at night looked in the wrong direction and was knocked down by an automobile—a moment, he later recalled, of a man aghast, a world aglare: "I do not understand why I was not broken like an eggshell or squashed like a gooseberry." Fourteen months later an American politician, sitting in an open car in Miami, Florida, was fired on by an assassin; the man beside him was hit. Those who believe that individuals make no difference to history might well ponder whether the next two decades would have been the same had Mario Contasini's car killed Winston Churchill in 1931 and Giuseppe Zangara's bullet killed Franklin Roosevelt in 1933. Suppose, in addition, that Adolf Hitler had been killed in the street fighting during the Munich *Putsch* of 1923 and that Lenin had died of typhus during the First World War. What would the 20th century be like now?

For better or for worse, individuals do make a difference. "The notion that a people can run itself and its affairs anonymously," wrote the philosopher William James, "is now well known to be the silliest of absurdities. Mankind does nothing save through initiatives on the part of inventors, great or small, and imitation by the rest of us—these are the sole factors in human progress. Individuals of genius show the way, and set the patterns, which common people then adopt and follow."

Leadership, James suggests, means leadership in thought as well as in action. In the long run, leaders in thought may well make the greater difference to the world. But, as Woodrow Wilson once said, "Those only are leaders of men, in the general eye, who lead in action. . . . It is at their hands that new thought gets its translation into the crude language of deeds." Leaders in thought often invent in solitude and obscurity, leaving to later generations the tasks of imitation. Leaders in action—the leaders portrayed in this series— have to be effective in their own time.

And they cannot be effective by themselves. They must act in response to the rhythms of their age. Their genius must be adapted, in a phrase of William James's, "to the receptivities of the moment." Leaders are useless without followers. "There goes the mob," said the French politician hearing a clamor in the streets. "I am their leader. I must follow them." Great leaders turn the inchoate emotions of the mob to purposes of their own. They seize on the opportunities of their time, the hopes, fears, frustrations, crises, potentialities.

They succeed when events have prepared the way for them, when the community is waiting to be aroused, when they can provide the clarifying and organizing ideas. Leadership ignites the circuit between the individual and the mass and thereby alters history.

It may alter history for better or for worse. Leaders have been responsible for the most extravagant follies and most monstrous crimes that have beset suffering humanity. They have also been vital in such gains as humanity has made in individual freedom, religious and racial tolerance, social justice and respect for human rights.

There is no sure way to tell in advance who is going to lead for good and who for evil. But a glance at the gallery of men and women in *World Leaders—Past and Present* suggests some useful tests.

One test is this: do leaders lead by force or by persuasion? By command or by consent? Through most of history leadership was exercised by the divine right of authority. The duty of followers was to defer and to obey. "Theirs not to reason why,/ Theirs but to do and die." On occasion, as with the so-called "enlightened despots" of the 18th century in Europe, absolutist leadership was animated by humane purposes. More often, absolutism nourished the passion for domination, land, gold and conquest and resulted in tyranny.

The great revolution of modern times has been the revolution of equality. The idea that all people should be equal in their legal condition has undermined the old structures of authority, hierarchy and deference. The revolution of equality has had two contrary effects on the nature of leadership. For equality, as Alexis de Tocqueville pointed out in his great study *Democracy in America*, might mean equality in servitude as well as equality in freedom.

"I know of only two methods of establishing equality in the political world," Tocqueville wrote. "Rights must be given to every citizen, or none at all to anyone . . . save one, who is the master of all." There was no middle ground "between the sovereignty of all and the absolute power of one man." In his astonishing prediction of 20th-century totalitarian dictatorship, Tocqueville explained how the revolution of equality could lead to the "*Führerprinzip*" and more terrible absolutism than the world had ever known.

But when rights are given to every citizen and the sovereignty of all is established, the problem of leadership takes a new form, becomes more exacting than ever before. It is easy to issue commands and enforce them by the rope and the stake, the concentration camp and the *gulag*. It is much harder to use argument and achievement to overcome opposition and win consent. The Founding Fathers of the United States understood the difficulty. They believed that history had given them the opportunity to decide, as

Alexander Hamilton wrote in the first Federalist Paper, whether men are indeed capable of basing government on "reflection and choice, or whether they are forever destined to depend . . . on accident and force."

Government by reflection and choice called for a new style of leadership and a new quality of followership. It required leaders to be responsive to popular concerns, and it required followers to be active and informed participants in the process. Democracy does not eliminate emotion from politics; sometimes it fosters demagoguery; but it is confident that, as the greatest of democratic leaders put it, you cannot fool all of the people all of the time. It measures leadership by results and retires those who overreach or falter or fail.

It is true that in the long run despots are measured by results too. But they can postpone the day of judgment, sometimes indefinitely, and in the meantime they can do infinite harm. It is also true that democracy is no guarantee of virtue and intelligence in government, for the voice of the people is not necessarily the voice of God. But democracy, by assuring the rights of opposition, offers built-in resistance to the evils inherent in absolutism. As the theologian Reinhold Niebuhr summed it up, "Man's capacity for justice makes democracy possible, but man's inclination to injustice makes democracy necessary."

A second test for leadership is the end for which power is sought. When leaders have as their goal the supremacy of a master race or the promotion of totalitarian revolution or the acquisition and exploitation of colonies or the protection of greed and privilege or the preservation of personal power, it is likely that their leadership will do little to advance the cause of humanity. When their goal is the abolition of slavery, the liberation of women, the enlargement of opportunity for the poor and powerless, the extension of equal rights to racial minorities, the defense of the freedoms of expression and opposition, it is likely that their leadership will increase the sum of human liberty and welfare.

Leaders have done great harm to the world. They have also conferred great benefits. You will find both sorts in this series. Even "good" leaders must be regarded with a certain wariness. Leaders are not demigods; they put on their trousers one leg after another just like ordinary mortals. No leader is infallible, and every leader needs to be reminded of this at regular intervals. Irreverence irritates leaders but is their salvation. Unquestioning submission corrupts leaders and demeans followers. Making a cult of a leader is always a mistake. Fortunately hero worship generates its own antidote. "Every hero," said Emerson, "becomes a bore at last."

The signal benefit the great leaders confer is to embolden the rest of us to live according to our own best selves, to be active, insistent, and resolute in affirming our own sense of things. For great leaders attest to the reality of human freedom against the supposed inevitabilities of history. And they attest to the wisdom and power that may lie within the most unlikely of us, which is why Abraham Lincoln remains the supreme example of great leadership. A great leader, said Emerson, exhibits new possibilities to all humanity. "We feed on genius. . . . Great men exist that there may be greater men."

Great leaders, in short, justify themselves by emancipating and empowering their followers. So humanity struggles to master its destiny, remembering with Alexis de Tocqueville: "It is true that around every man a fatal circle is traced beyond which he cannot pass; but within the wide verge of that circle he is powerful and free; as it is with man, so with communities."

—*New York*

1

The Making of a Legend

As dawn broke on the morning of January 8, 1815, Major General Andrew Jackson was standing on a mud-walled parapet five miles from the city of New Orleans. He was peering intently through fog and gloom toward a British camp that lay less than two miles away. Although only 47, Jackson was old beyond his years. His hair was long and gray, his body lean, almost gaunt, the result of chronic dysentery. A faded uniform of coarse blue cloth and yellow buckskin, a small cape wrapped around his bony shoulders, and great, unpolished boots that dwarfed his skinny legs were his only protection against the damp, freezing air. A stranger looking at him that morning would have found it hard to believe that Andrew Jackson was a great Indian fighter and military leader, but his soldiers knew him better. They loved this shabby man, whom they called "Old Hickory," for they knew that he possessed immense determination and an iron will that made him master of any situation.

On that morning, Old Hickory was facing the greatest challenge of his life. Arrayed before him was an overwhelming force of British regulars, more

The War of 1812 ends with a British-American handshake in Ghent, Belgium, on December 24, 1814. News of the conclusion of the treaty did not reach America until shortly after Jackson's forces had gained a victory over the British at New Orleans on January 8, 1815.

Andrew Jackson (1767–1845) at the Battle of New Orleans in 1815. The artist has given the general a much more elegant uniform than he or his men really wore. The smartly dressed British troops—"redcoats" to the Americans—called the often threadbare U.S. troops "dirty shirts."

Mortally wounded during a battle with the British frigate HMS *Shannon*, Captain James Lawrence (right; 1781–1813) collapses on the deck of the USS *Chesapeake*. The American hero's legendary last words—"Don't give up the ship!"—became a popular slogan during the War of 1812.

than 6,000 seasoned veterans, many of them fresh from battlefields in Europe, where they had fought bitter campaigns against the armies of Emperor Napoleon of France. Their commander was Lieutenant General Sir Edward Pakenham, a brilliant strategist who was considered one of the British army's best officers. The British, their slogan "booty and beauty," planned to capture New Orleans and hold it, either to force favorable concessions at the peace negotiations then under way in the Belgian city of Ghent, or to give Britain a permanent foothold in the American Southwest. Whoever controlled New Orleans controlled the Mississippi Valley; a British victory could thus thwart the territorial ambitions of the United States. What neither army knew before the awful battle that was to be fought that day was that a peace treaty ending the War of 1812 had been signed in Ghent more than two weeks earlier.

(The War of 1812 was named for the year of its commencement. The United States had gone to war

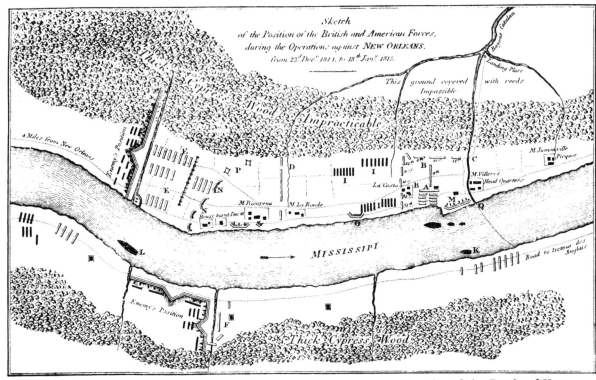

Sketch of the Position of the British and American Forces, during the Operations against NEW ORLEANS. From 23rd Decr 1814, to 18th Janr 1815.

with Britain in response to a number of provocations, the most blatant of which was the British navy's forcible impressment of American merchant seamen into service aboard its own vessels. The British had initiated this policy when the French, with whom Britain had been at war for several years, began to seize all vessels that traded with Britain. Lacking sufficient seamen to cope with the escalation of the war at sea, the Royal Navy began to waylay American shipping, ostensibly to search for British deserters. However, many of the "deserters" abducted by the British were nothing of the kind. They were often Americans, both native-born and naturalized. Another cause of the war was the western states' resentment of the fact that British diplomats and agents based in Canada had supported the Indians of the Ohio Valley in their war against encroaching American settlers.)

All that stood between the British and New Orleans on this fateful day in the period between the signing of the Treaty of Ghent and news of its conclusion reaching America's shores, was Jackson's army—if it could be called that. Except for a few

The site of the Battle of New Orleans. Because the War of 1812 had officially ended two weeks before the battle took place, the victory that Jackson's forces gained at New Orleans had no military value. It did, however, set off an explosion of patriotism, and made Jackson the most popular American hero since George Washington (1732–1799), first president of the United States.

regulars, it was a motley array of militiamen, backwoodsmen, pirates, Indians, and free blacks. Some people had disliked Jackson's decision to arm 200 freedmen—it might give slaves the wrong ideas—but General Jackson, a slaveholder himself, stood firm against his critics. "The free men of color," he asserted, "would make excellent soldiers." He ordered that the black recruits were to be treated and paid exactly like the other volunteers.

The Americans' only advantage was their defensive position, an earthen rampart that stretched 1,000 yards from the banks of the Mississippi River on the right of their line to an almost impenetrable swamp on their left. In fact, the odds against Jackson seemed so fearsome that members of the Louisiana legislature had suggested he surrender without a fight in return for a British promise not to destroy the city. Old Hickory had scuttled that notion with characteristic decisiveness. He told the governor "to blow them up," if the legislators persisted with such ideas.

Jackson had no intention of surrendering to anyone, much less the British, whom he hated passionately. Some might say he had cause for this hatred. The British had been responsible for the deaths of his mother and two brothers, and on his own head he bore a scar from a British saber, received when, as a young boy, he had refused to clean the boots of an officer. The British might defeat his army; they would never defeat him.

Nevertheless, even the indomitable Jackson must have had some doubts during the weeks preceding the confrontation at New Orleans. From the moment he had learned of the British intentions in the Southwest, he had been constantly on the move, shoring up defenses here, sending soldiers there, always trying to anticipate the enemy's main point of attack.

After repulsing a thrust at Mobile, where he gave the British "bloody noses," Jackson had hurried to New Orleans, which was rumored to be their next target. Arriving on December 1, 1814, Old Hickory was shocked to find the city completely unprepared for hostilities despite the fact that rumors of an impending British invasion had been circulating for weeks. New Orleans lacked adequate defenses, weapons, and manpower. Jackson immediately appealed to neighboring states for reinforcements, but he lost valuable time assembling a force capable of coping with the thousands of regulars the British were expected to field.

To make matters worse, many of the men who answered his call arrived without adequate clothing or weapons. For example, of the 2,400 Kentuckians who came racing to his aid, only 700 had rifles. "I do not believe it," groaned Jackson. "I have never seen a Kentuckian without a gun and a pack of cards and a bottle of whiskey in my life." The women of New Orleans solved the clothing problem by making hundreds of overcoats out of blankets, but Jackson never did find enough guns to go around. Fortunately, he was able to obtain the services of a band of pirates led by the notorious Lafitte brothers. The pirates, who were a law unto themselves, controlled a section of the Louisiana coast known as Barataria and made their livelihood preying on Spanish vessels. These brigands may have been better suited to the city jail, but Jackson welcomed them into his army because they were expert cannoneers and came well armed.

Despite these frantic efforts to defend New Orleans, the British almost captured it by surprise. Jackson had ordered that every approach to the city be guarded and blockaded, but the British found an unprotected *bayou* (a marshy creek) and used it to land 1,800 men within eight miles of the city. Shocked and enraged—"By the Eternal, they shall not sleep on our soil"—Jackson ordered an immediate attack. Neither side gained the upper hand in the subsequent skirmish, but Jackson's assault forced the British to call for reinforcements from their fleet, which was anchored 60 miles away. While the British waited for their new troops, the Americans, assisted by hundreds of slaves, worked around the clock to erect a dirt wall along the edge of a dry canal roughly 12 feet wide and four feet deep. Within 24 hours the wall was finished, and behind it crouched some 4,000 men—the bulk of

When Jackson's battlefield leadership catapulted him into the national political arena, he was incredulous. "Do they think I am such a damned fool as to think myself fit for president of the United States?" he said in 1821. "I can command a body of men," the old soldier added, "but I am not fit for president."

Jackson's army—supported by perhaps a dozen cannon. Another 1,000 men were held in reserve, occupying positions in the rear.

For more than two weeks the armies had confronted each other, and now the long-awaited assault was at hand. At about 1:00 A.M., scouts had awakened Old Hickory to inform him of unusual activity in the enemy camp. He immediately roused his officers and then spent the rest of the night inspecting the defenses and encouraging the troops. When a rocket lit the dark sky at about 6:00 A.M., he calmly remarked: "That, I believe, is their signal to advance."

For several minutes the anxious Americans saw nothing. Only the skirling of bagpipes and the beating of drums told Jackson's army that the British were advancing. Suddenly, a gust of wind briefly cleared the morning fog, revealing the enemy, less than 600 yards away, approaching in two massive columns across a frost-covered field. It was a breathtaking sight: seemingly endless rows of red-coated soldiers, their bayonets at the ready. Even more impressive were the 900 men of the 93rd Scots Highlanders, each at least six feet tall, marching in time to their pipers' tunes.

"Fire!" shouted Jackson, and the wall erupted with orange flame. The British were too far away for the muskets, but the cannonballs cut gaping furrows through their massed ranks. The columns paused, reformed, and came forward at a run.

"Load! Aim! Fire!" The British fell in scarlet heaps, but still they pressed home their attack. Those in the rear hurdled the bodies of their fallen comrades only to be cut down themselves.

Much went wrong for the British on that terrible morning. One assault group was to have crossed the Mississippi, captured an American artillery battery there, and then turned the cannon on the Americans across the river. However, that group was swept downstream by the river's swift current and thus out of position when the attack began. The main assault was bungled even more. It was to have been led by 300 soldiers carrying scaling ladders and bundles of sugar cane with which to fill the dry canal, but when the signal to attack was given, these men were not in place either. Thus, the soldiers who reached the canal were unable to climb the wall, and were exposed to intense musket and cannon fire from above. Some tried to cut steps in the dirt wall with their bayonets, but the few who managed to get into the American lines were either killed or captured.

One of those who died that morning was Lieutenant General Pakenham, the British commander. When he saw his assault begin to fail, Pakenham galloped to the head of the column and begged his retreating troops to halt and reform. At that point, a burst of grapeshot slashed his leg open and killed his horse, but he mounted another and continued to urge his men to attack. Even when struck a second time, Pakenham refused to concede. His last words were, "Order up the reserves!" They never appeared; the officers still on their feet knew the day was lost.

The engagement at New Orleans had been not a battle but a slaughter. The British suffered 291

British troops in action against Jackson's forces at New Orleans. Advancing across open ground, the courageous and superbly trained redcoats were helpless before the withering fire raining down upon them from Jackson's army's fortified positions. Panicked, the British retreated as the Americans' band played "Hail Columbia!"

dead, 1,262 wounded, and 484 captured (many of these were also wounded). The officers had suffered the worst attrition; three of four generals and eight colonels were either killed or wounded. One regiment lost 24 commissioned and noncommissioned officers, including its colonel and 12 sergeants.

Jackson reported his losses as seven killed and six wounded. Although he was not a religious man,

The death of Lieutenant General Sir Edward Pakenham (foreground center, being aided by colleagues; 1778–1815), commander of the British forces at the Battle of New Orleans. The flags in the background mark the ramparts from which Jackson's men raked the British troops with deadly fire.

His [Jackson's] stern, inflexible adherence to Democratic principles, his unwavering devotion to his country, and his intrepid opposition to her enemies, have so long thwarted their unhallowed schemes of ambition and power, that they fear the potency of his name on earth, even after his spirit shall have ascended to heaven.
—STEPHEN DOUGLAS
Illinois congressman,
writing in 1844

Jackson had a simple explanation for the astounding disproportion: "The unerring hand of Providence," he said, "shielded my men." Whatever the explanation for this remarkable victory, one thing is certain: Jackson's life had been merely a preface to this moment, for the Battle of New Orleans swept him to the presidency and marked him for immortality.

2
An Officer's Boots

Andrew Jackson, the third son of Irish immigrants, was a product of the frontier. He was born on March 15, 1767, in the Waxhaws, the harsh pine-barren region along the border between North Carolina and South Carolina. His father, for whom he was named, had died while building a log cabin a month before Andrew's birth. His mother, Elizabeth Hutchinson Jackson, was a pious woman who prayed that Andrew would become a Presbyterian minister. The young man, however, showed no inclination toward such a career. He was bright enough, but he was more ruffian than gentleman, his ferocious temper a match for his crackling blue eyes and his bright red hair.

No one who knew him ever forgot that temper. It dominated his personality and could make brave men quake. When he was angry—which was often—his blue eyes would harden, his face would flush, his body would shake, and he would unleash a torrent of oaths. To those around him, it seemed he must burst a blood vessel or have a stroke. His friends, however, claimed that Jackson faked these tantrums in order to get his way when other methods failed, and that actually he was always in control of himself.

Near his early home in the Waxhaws (a region on the border between North Carolina and South Carolina), young Andrew Jackson surveys the chaos following a surprise British raid in 1780. The "Waxhaw Massacre," which took the lives of 113 patriot soldiers, greatly intensified Jackson's hatred of the British.

Jackson's first home, a log cabin in the Waxhaws. Jackson always identified himself as a South Carolinian, but the exact location of the house where he was born has never been determined. Today, both North Carolina and South Carolina claim to be his birthplace.

Young Andrew received the best education the frontier community could provide, but no one would have mistaken him for a scholar. He did not like to read, never mastered spelling, and was often ungrammatical in his speech and writing. Nonetheless, he would prove to be an eloquent and persuasive man, able to stir others to seemingly impossible feats.

A major force in his life was his hatred for the British. Formed by stories his mother told of the family's suffering under British rule in Ireland, it was fixed by his own experiences during the American Revolution. The Waxhaws became a battle-

A British officer prepares to attack 13-year-old Andrew Jackson, who had enraged him by refusing to polish his boots. The future president of the United States carried the scars of this encounter for the rest of his life.

Spectators at a cockfight, one of the several types of sporting event that Andrew Jackson greatly enjoyed. Even among other rowdy, hard-drinking young frontiersmen, Jackson managed to stand out. "He was such a rake," recalled one neighbor, "that my husband would not bring him into the house!"

ground in the struggle for independence as Tories (British loyalists) and patriots fought a vicious civil war within the broader context of the war against Britain. It was neighbor against neighbor, sometimes even parent against child.

Caught up in the strife, the Jackson family paid a fearful price for its patriotism. The eldest son, Hugh, had already died fighting the British when Andrew and his brother Robert were captured following a skirmish. A Tory neighbor had reported their hiding place to British dragoons. While some of the dragoons were ransacking the house in which the brothers had been hiding, a British officer ordered Andrew to clean his boots. The 13-year-old boy, demonstrating the spirit and courage that were to mark his entire life, refused. "Sir, I am a prisoner of war, and claim to be treated as such," he said calmly. For that bit of insolence the officer slashed at Andrew's head with his sword. Only the boy's upraised hand, which was cut to the bone, saved his life.

The dragoons took the Jackson boys to a prison about 40 miles away. There they both fell seriously ill, the result of hunger, infected wounds, and smallpox, which they caught from the other prisoners. Elizabeth Jackson, who had been searching for her boys, finally found them and arranged for their release through an exchange of prisoners. She brought them home, but it was too late for Robert, who died a short time later. Andrew was critically ill for several weeks. When he finally seemed on the road to recovery, his mother went to Charleston, South Carolina, where she ministered to sick relatives confined aboard British prison ships in the harbor. Before she left, she gave Andrew some advice. "None will respect you more than you respect yourself," she said. "Avoid quarrels as long as you can . . . but sustain your manhood always. Never bring a suit in law for . . . defamation. The law offers no remedy for such outrages that can satisfy the feelings of a true man." Andrew Jackson never saw his mother again. She died of cholera, caught while nursing the prisoners, leaving her son a 14-year-old orphan.

For the next three years, young Andrew lived with relatives and enjoyed a wild, reckless life. He picked up habits—not all of them good—that never left him. He loved to gamble, especially on cockfights and horse races. But he was also ambitious. When he reached the age of 17, he decided it was time to make something of his life; the profession he chose as the path to wealth and respectability was law. Packing his few belongings, he moved to Salisbury, North Carolina, about 75 miles from the Waxhaws, where he studied law, first in the office of Spruce McCay and then with the firm of Colonel John Stokes. A flamboyant and successful lawyer, Stokes sported a silver knob in place of one of his hands, which had been lost in war. He wielded the knob like a gavel during arguments before the bar.

The two years that Jackson spent in Salisbury prepared him to practice law; they also prepared him to excel at less lofty pursuits. According to one Salisbury resident, he was the "most roaring, rollicking, game-cocking, horse-racing, card-playing, mischievous fellow" in town. The accuracy of this view was confirmed, years later, by the expressions of shock that emanated from the people of Salisbury when Jackson ran for president of the United States. "What!" marveled one woman, "Jackson up for president? If he can be president, anybody can!"

Actually, Jackson did more than get into trouble during his two years in Salisbury; on September 26, 1787, two judges certified him qualified to practice law. Because the area offered few opportunities to an aspiring lawyer, Jackson once again packed his belongings and struck out for a new life, this time heading west. His destination was Nashville, a new community being carved out of the western wilderness.

Fort Nashborough, one of the few buildings that comprised the frontier community of Nashville when Jackson arrived there in 1788. The fort, whose replica stands in the center of Nashville (now the capital of Tennessee), was built in 1779 to protect the early settlers from attacks by Indians.

3

Judge Jackson

After a 300-mile journey and a series of adventures that included escaping from hostile Cherokee Indians and the killing of a panther that had attempted to make a meal of one of his horses, Jackson reached Nashville in October 1788. A frontier community on the banks of the Cumberland River, Nashville consisted of a rickety stockade, a cluster of log cabins, and a roughhewn courthouse about 18 feet square, where the young lawyer hoped to build a thriving practice. For his residence, Jackson chose a blockhouse some 10 miles away; it was owned by a widow named Mrs. Rachel Stockley Donelson, who enjoyed considerable social prominence in the area.

The Donelson home was a long way from the county seat, but it had its compensations. One of them was the widow's young and vivacious daughter, Rachel, who was married to a violently jealous man named Lewis Robards. Jackson quickly fell in love with the bewitching Rachel, whose husband left her soon after the young lawyer took up residence in the Donelson household. Thinking that Robards had divorced Rachel, Jackson married her, only to discover a short time later that there had been no

Rachel Donelson Robards Jackson (c. 1766–1828) married Andrew Jackson twice: in 1791, when she mistakenly believed she had a legal divorce from her first husband; and in 1794, when the divorce was actually granted.

At age 62, Jackson was still carrying the bullets he had received in duels that he fought in 1806 and 1813. When he was 65, doctors relieved the constant pain in his arm by removing the bullet he had taken in 1813, but the other, near his heart, was to be a permanent burden.

divorce. Eventually, Robards did obtain his divorce, and Rachel and Andrew were legally married. However, the confused circumstances of their courtship and marriage were to haunt the couple for years, as gossips and political enemies continually circulated malicious rumors about the manner in which Jackson won his lady's heart.

Despite its controversial aspects, Jackson's marriage proved beneficial to his career because the Donelsons were a wealthy and respected family. Records show that the young lawyer handled as many as half the court cases in the district in the years following his arrival in Nashville. Since money was scarce, he often accepted land as payment for his legal fees, thereby becoming an important landowner. In time, Jackson bought a tract of 650 acres near Nashville; this was to be the site for his magnificent plantation and mansion, the Hermitage.

While successfully pursuing his legal career, Jackson became active in local politics. He was appointed attorney general of Tennessee's Mero District in 1791. When Tennessee was admitted to the Union in 1796, he was elected its first delegate to the U.S. House of Representatives. His early congressional record was not inspiring, however. He was the only representative to vote against giving George Washington a tribute when he stepped down from the presidency in 1796. Jackson later said he had voted "nay" because he had disapproved of the 1794 Jay Treaty, under which Britain had evacuated several American forts in return for concessions by the United States.

Jackson's contrary vote later embarrassed him politically because some people thought that anyone who had voted against "the father of his country" should not himself be president. His negative vote did not, however, hurt his popularity in Tennessee, which elected him to the U.S. Senate in 1797. Finding the duties of a senator unexciting, Jackson soon resigned to accept an appointment to the Superior Court of Tennessee at a salary of $600 a year. This high salary enable him to develop his plantation and to pursue a number of extremely profitable financial enterprises.

Judge Jackson remained on the bench for six

years. Although his long black gown made him look properly judicial, his legal opinions were not exactly models of jurisprudence. According to one observer, they were "short, technical, unlearned, sometimes ungrammatical"—but "generally right."

During these years, Judge Jackson's wealth and reputation grew steadily. It was also during this period that Jackson increased his reputation as a duelist and brawler. Because of his temper, he was quick to take insult and even quicker to demand satisfaction. The number of duels he fought is uncertain, but it is known that there would have been

Three decades after he arrived in Nashville, Jackson built the stately mansion he named the Hermitage. He expected it to be a quiet retreat (a hermitage is the home of a hermit, or recluse), but its spacious rooms were always to be filled with visiting relatives, friends, clergymen, admirers, and politicians.

more had they not been prevented by the intercession of friends or the change of heart of his
opponents.

Jackson's notorious 1806 duel with a speculator
and slavetrader named Charles Dickinson, like
many of his fights, involved his marriage to Rachel.
The affair started with a misunderstanding over a
bet, and escalated into a duel when Dickinson made
the mistake of maligning Rachel's reputation. Despite the fact that Dickinson was considered the
best pistol shot in Tennessee, Jackson did not hes-
itate to challenge him. The two met across the state
line in Kentucky.

Jackson's cool appraisal of the probable course of
the impending duel, in which the odds were undoubtedly against him, reveals much about his complex personality and his courage. Conceding
Dickinson's superiority as a marksman, Jackson

Practicing his own brand of law, Judge Andrew Jackson commands a gunman named Russell Bean to drop his pistols outside a Tennessee courthouse. Bean, who had threatened to kill the first man to approach him, later explained why he had obeyed Jackson. "I looked him in the eye," said Bean, "and I saw 'shoot.'"

recognized that his opponent would almost certainly shoot first and that he was unlikely to miss. Jackson gambled that the wound would not be fatal and that he would then be able to take his time with his return shot.

As Jackson had anticipated, Dickinson fired first. A puff of dust from Jackson's shirt indicated that the shot had been accurate. Instead of falling, however, Jackson merely put one hand over his chest and slowly raised his pistol with the other hand. Taking careful aim at his horrified adversary, he pulled the trigger. The pistol failed to fire. Slowly, Jackson recocked it and aimed again. Dickinson was aghast; he had no choice but to remain at his mark and await his fate. This time the pistol fired; the ball hit below the ribs, and Dickinson bled to death within a few minutes.

Actually, Jackson was seriously wounded. Only

his loose garments, which had caused Dickinson to misjudge his shot, had saved Jackson's life. Even at that, Jackson nearly bled to death. As he had been calmly taking aim, his boots had been filling with blood. In fact, Dickinson's ball had lodged so close to his heart that the doctors were afraid to remove it. Jackson carried the ball in his chest for the rest of his life. When, shortly after the duel, someone remarked on his luck in being able to shoot Dickinson despite such a serious wound, Jackson retorted: "I should have hit him, if he had shot me through the brain."

A few years later Jackson was involved in another celebrated, near-fatal encounter. This time, one of his friends, William Carroll, was challenged to a duel by Jesse Benton, brother of the future Missouri senator, Thomas Hart Benton. When Carroll asked Jackson to be his second, Jackson at first refused and tried to get the men to resolve their differences without a duel. When this effort failed, he reluctantly agreed to be Carroll's second and the duel— if it can be called that—took place. Benton fired first, missed, and then tried to run away, whereupon Carroll shot him in the seat of his pants. The wound was not serious, but it was very embarrassing. When Thomas Hart Benton heard that Jackson had been involved in his brother's humiliation, he issued a challenge of his own in very disrespectful language. Jackson, in turn, responded that duels were only for gentlemen and promised to horsewhip Thomas Hart Benton when he found him.

As luck would have it, Jackson encountered the Bentons one day in Nashville while going to the post office to get his mail. Jackson shouted: "Now, you rascal, I am going to punish you. Defend yourself!" When Thomas Benton reached into his pocket, Jackson thought he was getting a pistol, so he drew his own gun. As Benton backed away, his brother Jesse, who was standing in a doorway, shot Jackson at point blank range. One ball shattered his left shoulder; another broke his left arm and lodged near the bone. The doctors thought they would have to amputate the arm, but before he lost consciousness, Jackson ordered: "I shall keep my arm!"

Politician Thomas Hart Benton (1782–1858), who was involved in a duel between his brother Jesse and Jackson in 1813, later became a senator from Missouri and Jackson's staunch political ally. Benton was often called "Old Bullion" because, like Jackson, he strongly advocated "hard" currency—gold or silver bullion.

Jackson kept his arm—and his life—but it had been another close call. As for the Bentons, they decided to leave Nashville, certain that their lives would be forfeit once Jackson recovered. Thomas Hart Benton ended up in Missouri, where he served as a U.S. senator for 30 years; ironically, he became one of Jackson's most enthusiastic political supporters.

At this point in his life, Jackson's was a personality of almost bewildering diversity. Although he was a successful planter and an office holder of some standing, he was also a gambler, brawler, and duelist. He was kind to those dear to him and loyal to a fault, but he could not forgive an injury or an insult. Indeed, he was an implacable foe whose vocabulary did not include the word "defeat." These may not have been ideal qualities for a politician, but they were certainly appropriate for a military leader—which is what Jackson was soon to become. In fact, military service was to be the turning point in the life of this complex and driven man.

4
General Jackson

Andrew Jackson became major general of the Tennessee militia in 1802. He attained this position through an election that he won, not on the basis of his military experience or training—because he had none—but because he was a shrewd and popular politician as well as a personal friend of the governor, Archibald Roane. The election had ended in a tie between Jackson and another popular Tennessean, John Sevier, a hero of the American Revolution and a former governor of the state. Nonetheless, Roane chose Jackson over Sevier to lead the state militia.

Despite his obvious lack of qualifications for the post, Jackson proved to be an exceptional leader of men. His entanglement in the famous Burr Conspiracy, however, almost ruined his military career at its outset. Aaron Burr had served as vice-president of the United States from 1801 to 1805, but he was probably better known for the 1804 duel in which he killed former U.S. Secretary of the Treasury Alexander Hamilton. Nevertheless, Jackson was probably flattered when the urbane and sophisticated Burr visited him at the Hermitage and outlined his plans for an expedition into the South-

The political philosophy of Alexander Hamilton (1755–1804), the first U.S. secretary of the treasury, was the exact opposite of Andrew Jackson's. The deeply conservative Hamilton believed that the nation should be governed by its wealthy landowners; Jackson insisted that all American citizens, regardless of their economic status, should enjoy equal political rights.

Jackson, who was tall (6 feet, 1 inch) and gaunt (145 pounds), carried himself ramrod-straight. He had a lean face, clear blue eyes, and thick, iron-gray hair. The quintessential American frontiersman, he was the only first-generation president of the United States; all his forebears were foreign-born.

west that would, he said, drive the Spanish away from the American frontier. As a militia commander, Jackson would have been invaluable to Burr, if he could be won to his cause. Moreover, Jackson was an intense nationalist who had often demonstrated his disregard for the fine points of international law.

Burr's scheme, however, proved to be not only foolhardy but treasonous. Burr, who claimed to have secret permission for his audacious plan from

Alexander Hamilton (right) and U.S. Vice-President Aaron Burr (1756–1836) prepare to fight a duel in Weehawken, New Jersey, on July 11, 1804. Hamilton, who disapproved of dueling and only accepted Burr's challenge to prove his own courage, deliberately missed his target. Burr, however, shot to kill, and Hamilton, struck in the chest, died the next day.

President Thomas Jefferson, had actually been given no such permission. Had Jackson cooperated in Burr's proposed venture, he would have suffered political disgrace. Certainly, the people in the West would have welcomed removal of the Spanish threat from their borders, and Jackson was a westerner as well as a nationalist. Only after learning that Major General James Wilkinson, then governor of the Louisiana Territory and a man of extremely dubious reputation, was involved with Burr did Jackson be-

> *[It] is not in a splendid government, supported by powerful monopolies and aristocratical establishments, that [my countrymen] will find happiness, or their liberties protected, but in a plain system, void of pomp— protecting all, and granting favors to none.*
> —ANDREW JACKSON

come suspicious. The fact that Wilkinson's reputation was entirely deserved became apparent later, when it was revealed that he was a paid agent of Spain while employed by the United States. Historians still do not know the details of Burr and Wilkinson's plan, but it may have included the establishment of a separate country in the land they expected to take from the Spanish. Regardless of his suspicions, Jackson did help Burr by building two troop-transport boats and by purchasing supplies. Not until several months later did Jackson learn that there were no secret orders from the president.

When Burr was arrested and tried for treason in 1807, Jackson testified on his behalf. He denied knowing that Burr had planned any treasonous activities. This is undoubtedly true. Jackson was too patriotic an American to have been part of a treasonous conspiracy. What seems more plausible is that he did not know the true extent of Burr's intentions.

Although Burr was acquitted, Jackson's defense of him angered the Jefferson administration and kept him from receiving a command when the War of 1812 broke out a few years later. He found himself an impatient and bitter spectator in the opening months of what is sometimes called America's second war of independence.

Jackson, of course, had offered his sword and the services of his Tennessee volunteers to the federal government as soon as hostilities broke out between the United States and Great Britain. In return he received only a curt letter from the secretary of war, accepting his offer but assigning him no command.

When he eventually did receive orders—in December 1812—they were to support Major General Wilkinson, who had been instructed to defend New Orleans in the event of a British invasion from the south. James Madison, who was president at that time, also intended that Jackson's force should eventually be employed in a strike against Spanish-held East Florida.

Jackson was excited by the prospect of finally avenging his own and his family's mistreatment at

Citizens! Who are we? and for what are we going to fight? are we the titled Slaves of [the king of England]? the military conscripts of [Emperor] Napoleon [of France]? No—we are the citizens of the only republic now existing in the world. . . . We are going to fight for the reestablishment of our national character, for the protection of our maritime citizens, to vindicate our right to a free trade, and, in fine, to seek some indemnity for past injuries, and some security against future aggressions.
—ANDREW JACKSON
in an 1812 proclamation
calling for volunteers to
fight the British after the
U.S. Congress had
authorized the enlistment
of 50,000 soldiers

the hands of the British during the War of Independence. By January 7, 1813, his forces were assembled and ready to start upon the first leg of the expedition to New Orleans. The cavalry and mounted infantry left Nashville that same day for the Mississippi Territory town of Natchez, where Jackson and the infantry, who were to travel by boat, would rendezvous with them in February. The 39-day, 1,000-mile journey down the Ohio River, which was clogged with ice in many places, proved both difficult and dangerous. Upon arriving in Natchez, Jackson, much to his disgust and dismay, found orders from Wilkinson requesting that he halt his advance and await further instructions.

Jackson and his army languished in Natchez until mid-March, when he received new orders—this time from John Armstrong, the secretary of war. Armstrong's letter thanked Jackson and his men

Heading for the Pacific coast in 1805, explorers Meriwether Lewis (1774–1809) and William Clark (1770–1838) confer with their guide, a Shoshone Indian woman named Sacajawea (c. 1786–1812). Lewis and Clark's expedition provided valuable information about the Louisiana Territory, the huge, uncharted area acquired by the United States in 1803.

for their services to date and ordered them to disband and return home. The only explanation offered was that the original reasons for the expedition no longer applied.

Jackson was shocked. In the East, the armed forces of the United States were losing battle after battle to the British, yet his men had not only had no opportunity to fight for their country, they were being dismissed with nothing more than a "thank you" from the politicians in Washington—whom Jackson had considered a collection of "old grannies" ever since their failure to request his services at the outbreak of war. Jackson suspected it was a plot to embarrass him, prompted by Wilkinson, who had managed to avoid being tainted by the Burr Conspiracy. Wilkinson and his allies, thought Jackson, probably assumed that Jackson's men would enlist in Wilkinson's army rather than attempt to

The USS *Constitution* defeats the British frigate HMS *Guerrière* (left) on August 19, 1812. While American land forces were being badly mauled in the early part of the War of 1812, the U.S. Navy's fast frigates scored numerous victories over the British at sea.

Aaron Burr's enthusiastic support for U.S. territorial expansion made him a hero to most westerners, who even approved of his killing Alexander Hamilton, a staunch defender of eastern interests, in a duel in 1804. In 1807 Burr was arrested and tried for treason, earning nationwide notoriety as a traitor despite the fact that he was acquitted.

return home without food, transportation, or money.

Jackson's reaction to Armstrong's letter was typical of his tendency to ascribe his problems and misfortunes to the machinations of hidden enemies. The angry Tennessean had no way of knowing that his seemingly humiliating circumstances had nothing to do with Wilkinson. What *had* happened was that the Madison administration had failed to gain congressional support for an invasion of East Florida. The members of Congress were convinced that the Spanish would consider any American move into that territory a declaration of war. They

A Creek Indian war party slaughters hundreds of settlers—men, women, and children—at Fort Mims, in the Mississippi Territory, in 1813, setting in motion a fearful tide of revenge that would eventually lead to their annihilation by the U.S. military. Appalling savagery was practiced by both whites and Indians in their long struggle for control of American land.

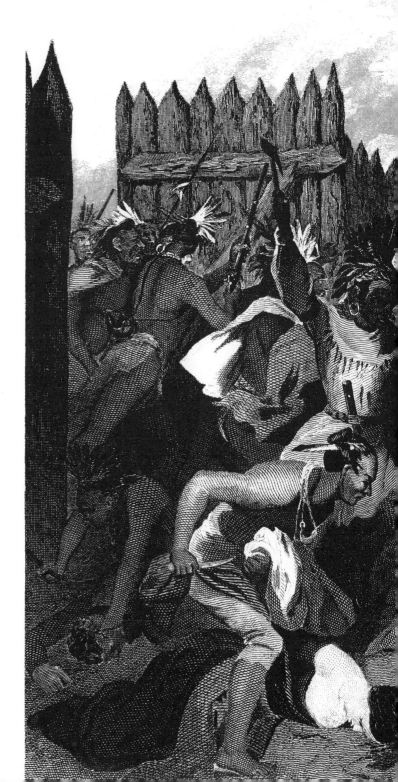

These brave men deserve a better fate and return from their government. At the call of their country they voluntarily rallied round its insulted standard. They followed me to the field; I shall carefully march them back to their homes.

—ANDREW JACKSON responding, in March 1813, to an order from Secretary of War John Armstrong telling him to dismiss his volunteers in Natchez, Mississippi

also believed that, since Spain was allied with Russia, whose emperor was trying to mediate the dispute between the United States and Britain, the administration's proposed venture would only aggravate an already complex international situation.

Unaware of the far-reaching ramifications of his dismissal, Jackson, acting on his own initiative and with the full support of his officers, decided that his men, having come to Natchez as a unit, would return home the same way. Many of them were ill and unable to walk, but Jackson had a remedy for the situation. The sick rode home on the horses be-

longing to the officers. Even Jackson walked.

It took the bedraggled volunteers two months to march back to Tennessee. To the rough militiamen under Jackson's command, he seemed as tough and resilient as hickory wood, and they began to call him "Old Hickory." It was the perfect name for this gritty campaigner, and he would bear it proudly in the military and political campaigns that lay ahead.

Despite the disappointment at Natchez, Old Hickory did not have long to wait for the action he craved. He learned that Creek Indians had killed some four hundred people at Fort Mims in the Mississippi Ter-

During the War of 1812, while Jackson marched south to fight the Spanish in Florida, the British were marching on Washington, D.C. On August 24, 1814, a British expeditionary force, under orders "to destroy and lay waste" American coastal cities, entered the nation's capital and burned all its public buildings, including the President's House.

British naval vessels bombard Fort McHenry, a key point in the defenses of Baltimore, Maryland, in September 1814. The Maryland state militia, whose members had been enraged by the British sacking of the nation's capital several weeks earlier, stood fast against the bombardment, finally forcing a British withdrawal on September 14.

ritory. The Creeks had joined forces with the famous Shawnee leader Tecumseh and were aiding the British in the War of 1812. Called "Red Sticks" for the color of their war clubs, the Creek militants greatly resented the white people who were settling in their country. The Creeks had valid complaints, but in those days few Americans recognized the Indians' claims to their ancestral lands.

Jackson immediately answered the call for revenge. He led his volunteers against the Creeks, waging a brutal, relentless campaign that forever destroyed their power.

Jackson inflicted the decisive blow against the Red Sticks at Horseshoe Bend, the militants' main village. A bend in the Tallapoosa River guarded the village on three sides; a log stockade ran along the fourth, and it was this section that Old Hickory attacked on the morning of March 27, 1814.

Unfortunately for the Creeks, the river that they had used as protection from their enemies proved to be their undoing, for once their log wall was

48

The Star-Spangled Banner flies above an American en-
campment. The U.S. flag became the subject of the country's national anthem ("The Star-Spangled Banner")
when a poem of the same name, written by American
patriot Francis Scott Key (1779–1843)—a veteran of the
War of 1812—and set to music by English composer
John Stafford Smith (1750–1836), was officially
adopted as the national anthem in 1931.

breached they could not retreat. By the end of the day, Jackson had won a spectacular victory against the Creeks, who had chosen death rather than surrender. Almost 900 Indians had been killed; Jackson's force suffered 47 dead and 75 wounded.

The Creeks had lost more than a battle. For his victory, Jackson was commissioned a major general in the U.S. Army by a grateful government and given command of the Seventh Military District of the United States (Tennessee, Louisiana, and the Mississippi Territory). Four months after the battle, Jackson called the Creek leaders together to negotiate a peace treaty. Known as the Treaty of Fort Jackson after the fort he built at the site, it forced the Creeks to surrender their claims to most of Alabama and part of Georgia. Not only did the treaty open a vast area of the West—some 23 million

Shawnee Indian chief Tecumseh (1768–1813) joined forces with the British after General (later president) William Henry Harrison (1773–1841) defeated his warriors at the Battle of Tippecanoe in 1811. Tecumseh, who had tried to form an Indian confederation to resist white expansion, was killed in a battle with Harrison's forces in October 1813.

In 1812 President Thomas Jefferson (1743–1826) ignored Jackson's offer to lead 2,500 volunteers into the war against the British. Jefferson remembered that Jackson had once been associated with Aaron Burr, whose trial for treasonable activities in 1807 had caused a major scandal from which few of Burr's colleagues emerged with their reputations untarnished.

acres—to settlement, it also made Old Hickory a great hero throughout the South and West.

Jackson followed this triumph with the even greater victory at New Orleans. By early 1815, when news of the Treaty of Ghent finally reached America and brought the War of 1812 to an end, Jackson had become a national hero and a legend in his own time.

But Jackson was not finished. In his opinion, the job of opening up the West remained incomplete. He had crushed the Creeks and embarrassed the

Creek Indian leader William Weatherford (c. 1780–1825), who had commanded the Creek attack on white settlers at Fort Mims in 1813, surrenders to Jackson at Horseshoe Bend in 1814. After the battle at Horsehoe Bend, which saw his forces decimated by Jackson's army, Weatherford asked Jackson to assist his tribe's women and children. Jackson promised that he would.

British, but the Spanish, who occupied Florida, still posed a threat to the United States. From the Spanish forts in Florida, hostile Indians obtained food, ammunition, and encouragement for their raids on American frontier settlements. Furthermore, the Spanish and their Seminole allies were giving sanctuary to runaway slaves.

As commander of the Seventh Military District, Jackson was dispatched by President James Monroe to punish the Indians and their Spanish friends in Florida. In December 1817 he led a 2,000-man army in search of the Seminole Indians who had recently massacred a boatload of American soldiers. Most of the Indians managed to hide in the swamps, but Jackson did seize St. Marks, one of the Spanish towns that had been supplying the Seminoles with food and equipment. There, he replaced the Spanish flag with the American flag. He also captured and hanged two British adventurers who had been training the Seminoles to fight. Wasting little time, Jackson moved on to capture Pensacola. By the end of May, he had overthrown the Spanish government in Florida and shipped its officials to Cuba. He then took it upon himself to claim the region for the United States, confident that Monroe would support his actions.

For once Old Hickory had miscalculated. Instead of submitting meekly to the fact of his conquest, Spain and Britain filed strong protests; to avert the threat of war, Monroe disavowed the actions of his overly zealous general and restored Florida to Spain. It was only a temporary setback, however, for on February 22, 1819, Spain sold Florida, together with all its lands east of the Mississippi and its claims in Oregon, to the United States for $5 million. As his reward, Jackson was named governor of Florida in 1821.

The late conduct of the Spanish government added to the hostile appearance and menacing attitude of their armed forces already encamped within the limits of our government, make it necessary that the militia under my command should be in complete order and at a moment's warning ready to march.
—ANDREW JACKSON calling for the mobilization of the Tennessee militia to support former Vice-President Aaron Burr's proposed western expedition, in a proclamation issued March 1806

In this 1813 drawing, entitled "Hunting Indians in Florida with bloodhounds," the artist has undoubtedly captured the brutality that characterized the behavior of many white settlers toward Indians during the 19th century. Jackson's invariably harsh and frequently murderous methods of "punishing" Florida's Seminoles led to their calling him "Sharp Knife."

5
Presidential Candidate

Following a brief term as governor of Florida, Andrew Jackson returned to his plantation in November 1821. Now in his mid-50s, he looked forward to a leisurely and carefree old age. His friends, however, had other plans for him. They were very much aware of his enormous popularity, and believed that he had a good chance of becoming president. Once the idea of running for the presidency had been planted, it found fertile soil; Old Hickory, the hero of New Orleans, was an ambitious man.

In aspiring to the presidency Jackson faced seemingly insurmountable obstacles. All the U.S. presidents so far had been polished and cultured individuals with considerable administrative experience. Each had been a member of the country's intellectual, social, and economic elite.

Jackson would be the first "self-made" man to reach the President's House, as it was then known. To get there, his support would have to come from what was called the common man, from people who had only recently become a powerful electoral voice.

An important step in Jackson's ambitious path to the presidency, which was being plotted by some of his political cronies, was to become a senator from

Leading American politician Henry Clay (1777–1852), to whom Jackson once referred as "the basest, meanest scoundrel that ever disgraced the image of God." Clay, whose detestation of Jackson was equally intense, once said of his rival, "I cannot believe that the killing of 2,000 Englishmen at New Orleans qualifies a person . . . for the presidency."

Senator Andrew Jackson, as portrayed by Ralph E. W. Earl in 1835. Many artists portrayed Jackson, but none was harder-working than Earl, who lived with the Jacksons for 17 years and painted numerous likenesses of the general. Although Earl's work was not popular with art critics, Jackson liked it; he paid Earl $50 for each of his portraits.

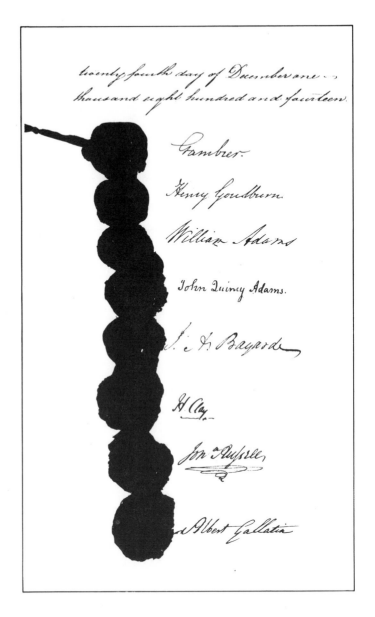

twenty-fourth day of December one-thousand eight hundred and fourteen.

Gambier.

Henry Goulburn.

William Adams

John Quincy Adams.

J. A. Bayard

H Clay

Jon Russell,

Albert Gallatin

Among the signatories to the Treaty of Ghent, which ended the War of 1812, were John Quincy Adams (1767–1848) and Henry Clay. The two trailed Jackson as vote-getters in the 1824 presidential election, but no contender had a majority. The contest was decided in Congress, which selected Adams to be the nation's sixth president.

Tennessee. How could he hope to win a national election, if he could not win one in his own state? This hurdle was crossed in October 1823, when he was appointed senator by the state legislature. As before, Jackson did not want to be a senator—"I am a senator against my wishes and feelings," he admitted—but he accepted the position at the urging of his advisers. However, it soon emerged that Jackson's becoming a senator might not have been as crucial to his presidential prospects as his advisers had imagined. When Jackson's presidential candidacy was announced, the news electrified the entire nation.

Jackson's competitors in the race for the presidency were the political giants of his day. Least known perhaps was Secretary of the Treasury William H. Crawford. The others, all prominent and respected leaders, were John C. Calhoun of South Carolina, spokesman for the South; Henry Clay, the speaker of the House of Representatives, who was known as "Harry of the West" and "the Great Pacificator"; and John Quincy Adams, of Massachusetts. Not only was Adams an eminent statesman in his own right (he and Clay had helped negotiate the Treaty of Ghent), he was also the son of the nation's second president, John Adams. The field of active candidates went from five to three when Calhoun withdrew in return for the promise of the vice-presidency and Crawford suffered a crippling stroke. Although Crawford refused to withdraw from the race, his chances of winning had been greatly diminished.

When the votes were counted in the fall of 1824, Jackson was found to have received the most: 155,800. Adams got 105,300, Clay 46,500, and Crawford 44,200. It was the vote in the electoral college, not the popular vote, that counted, however. But even there none of the candidates received a majority. Jackson, with 99, had a plurality. Of the others, Adams received 84, Crawford 41, Clay 37.

Since no one was a clear winner, the 12th Amendment to the Constitution required the House of Representatives to select the president from among the three candidates with the highest number of electoral votes. This automatically excluded Clay, and, with Crawford ill, the contest was now between Jackson and Adams.

Although out of the race himself, Clay now emerged as a key person in the contest. He was speaker of the House of Representatives and could thus exert tremendous influence on its deliberations. Moreover, Clay did not want to see Jackson

An overwhelming proportion of the material power of the Nation was against [Jackson]. The great media for the dissemination of information and the molding of public opinion fought him. Haughty and sterile intellectualism opposed him. Musty reaction disapproved him. Hollow and outworn traditionalism shook a trembling finger at him—all but the people of the United States.
—FRANKLIN D. ROOSEVELT
thirty-second president of
the United States (1933–1945)

elected president because he considered him too inexperienced for such an important position. That left Adams.

In what came to be called the "corrupt bargain," Clay supposedly asked his supporters in the House of Representatives to vote for Adams. In return for this favor, some people claimed, Adams made Clay his secretary of state.

That there may have been some sort of bargain seemed evident when the votes in the House were counted. Adams had received the votes of 13 states, Jackson 7, and Crawford 4. Adams was the new president.

Jackson was understandably disappointed. He had received the most votes in both the nation and

A crock commemorating Jackson's victory at the polls in the 1824 presidential election. The vote of the U.S. House of Representatives, which placed Adams in the White House instead of the more popular Jackson, infuriated Jackson's supporters. "Treachery, treachery!" shouted one congressman. "Damnable falsehood!"

the electoral college, yet he was not president. Nevertheless, he took his defeat with grace and dignity until he learned that Adams planned to make Clay his secretary of state, then he exploded: "So you see, the *Judas* of the West has closed his contract and will receive the thirty pieces of silver."

Jackson's conviction that there had been a "corrupt bargain" became the focus of attention among his supporters. In their opinion, Clay and Adams had conspired to deprive the American people of their choice for president. Old Hickory vowed to change things the next time around.

As a result of the controversy, interest in the next election swelled to immense proportions. By 1828, Jackson had had much time in which to reflect upon the lessons he had learned in 1824, and he

A cartoon from the presidential election campaign of 1828. In this campaign, John Quincy Adams's supporters accused Jackson of ordering countless military executions and of practicing "immoral ways." Jackson's supporters sometimes went to absurd lengths to refute the charges. "Gen. Jackson does not at any time play cards," one campaign statement said. "Neither does General Jackson swear."

was now prepared to do whatever was necessary to win. A key part of his campaign strategy was securing the assistance of Martin Van Buren, a short, stout, red-haired senator from New York, who had been dubbed the "Red Fox" and the "Little Magician" for his political wisdom. The wily Van Buren took over the management of Jackson's campaign and soon a new national party called the "democratic" party began to form around his political banner.

More people were eligible to vote in 1828 than had ever been the case before. Until the end of the 18th century an American's right to vote had depended upon his possessing a certain amount of property. However, during the first three decades of the 19th century the states had largely removed these property restrictions. The election of 1828, therefore, marks the beginning of modern politics. Until then, presidential elections had been rather gentlemanly affairs. Now, however, newspapers became heavily involved in the electoral process, and name-calling and mud-slinging intruded upon the discussion of issues, effectively discouraging the voters from forming opinions of the candidates based upon an appreciation of their merits and qualifications.

The 1828 campaign was also notable for introducing several features that became common in later presidential campaigns: the rallies, slogans, banners, and hoopla that are so much a part of American political life today. It was also one of the meanest presidential campaigns ever fought.

Widely distributed by Jackson's opponents during the presidential election campaign of 1828, the "coffin handbill" claimed that Jackson had shot six loyal soldiers in cold blood: in reality, the men were deserters and had been sentenced to death by a court-martial.

Some Account of some of the Bloody Deeds of
GEN. JACKSON.

Jacob Webb.   David Morrow.   John Harris.   Henry Lewis.   David Hunt.   Edward Lindsey.

A Jackson campaign poster of 1828 ridicules John Quincy Adams and calls his cabinet members "rats." "Old Hickory" (as Jackson had been known since 1813) is recommended as a "rod to whip out the rats" and other undesirables from the government. In a campaign that was characterized—to an extent that has never since been equalled—by violent personal abuse, this can be counted a relatively mild indictment.

Malicious personal attacks were the order of the day in this campaign. Although Adams was too dignified a person to encourage the things that were done on his behalf, he did little to stop them. Therefore, Jackson—and his wife—endured some of the most vicious character assassination ever suffered by a presidential candidate and his family. Jackson was accused of adultery for having married Rachel; his fondness for gambling and horse racing was publicized. Because he had once ordered some deserters from his army to be executed, his enemies published handouts known as "coffin handbills." These showed six black coffins, representing the executed soldiers, and, in bold type, purported to offer: "Some Account of Some of the Bloody Deeds of GENERAL JACKSON." For his friendship with Burr, he was accused of treason; for his duels, he was denounced as an irrational hothead. But the most damaging attacks were those that affected his beloved Rachel, who often broke down in tears over the things written about her in the newspapers. Jackson could endure the attacks against his own person, but the assaults on Rachel's character he found unbearable.

Meanwhile, Jackson's supporters were by no means innocent of slandering the opposition. Adams was accused of installing "gaming tables" in the President's House at public expense, of being a secret "monarchist," of padding his expense account, and even of supplying women for the tsar of Russia!

At the end of this degrading campaign, Jackson won a stunning victory. His popular vote was 648,273 to 508,064 for Adams. His electoral total was even more impressive—178 to 83. Jackson had broken the hold of the eastern elite on the President's House thanks to the largest voter turnout up to that time—more than twice as many people had gone to the polls in 1828 as had voted in 1824. The common man had spoken and Jackson was his choice. Jackson viewed the vote as a mandate for change, and he promised to make many. But in the moment of his greatest triumph, he also suffered his most crushing blow, the death of his wife.

The family was still at the Hermitage, preparing for the move to Washington, when Rachel suffered a crippling heart attack. The strain of the campaign, especially the assaults on her character, had taken a terrible toll. At first there was hope she would recover, but after lingering a few days, she died.

The shock was almost too much for Jackson. At first he refused to believe she was dead and remained at her side for hours. After burying Rachel in the garden of the Hermitage on Christmas Eve, 1828, he did nothing for days. Finally, accompanied by several friends and his nephew, Andrew Jackson Donelson, who was to become his private secretary, the grief-stricken Jackson began the long journey by steamboat and horseback to Washington. By the time he arrived in the capital, on February 11, the cheering crowds along the way had helped to restore his spirit, much to the relief of his family and friends.

Still mourning for his beloved wife, who had died at the end of 1828, a somber President-elect Jackson greets well-wishers on his way to Washington in early 1829. His decisive 1828 victory at the polls proved, his followers claimed, that he had been wrongfully denied the presidency in the previous election.

6
President Jackson

"There he is!" At these words, thousands of people surged forward to catch a glimpse of Old Hickory on inauguration day. "The shouting seemed to shake the ground," one man said. But the champion of the people seemed humble and subdued as he stood on the portico of the Capitol building, dwarfed by its enormous columns. Jackson bowed to the crowd and then took the oath of office from Chief Justice John Marshall. After kissing the Bible, Jackson read his inaugural address in a voice so low that only those standing near him could hear. His speech was short and skillful but not profound. He promised to protect the rights of the states, and to give everyone a chance to hold public office. Those who were incompetent or unfaithful he would remove.

Cannon salutes resounded through the city as Jackson then pushed his way through the crowd to mount his horse and ride to the President's House, where he planned to greet well-wishers informally. What occurred there has become an inauguration-day legend—"The reign of King Mob," one witness called it—as thousands of admirers thronged the President's House and its grounds. So heavy was

John C. Calhoun (1782–1850) of South Carolina was vice-president during Jackson's first term as president. Their relationship started well, but soon turned to bitter enmity. In 1837 Jackson said: "After eight years as president I have only two regrets: that I have not shot Henry Clay or hanged John C. Calhoun."

Andrew Jackson was the first "common man"—neither aristocratic nor an easterner—to attain the nation's highest office. America's poor loved him: he proved that a man born in a log cabin could become rich, win military honor—and be elected president of the United States.

Chief Justice John Marshall (1755–1835) administers the oath of office to Andrew Jackson on March 4, 1829. An immense crowd was on hand for the ceremony: eager to see the great event, 10,000 visitors from all over the country had converged on Washington, whose population was only 18,000.

the crush that Jackson had to sneak out a back door and take refuge in his hotel. Few of the revelers seemed to notice his absence, however; they were more concerned with enjoying the food and drink. In the process, they broke glasses and china, muddied the elegant furniture and rugs with their boots, and caused thousands of dollars worth of damage to the presidential residence. Only after the waiters took the food outside did the crowd vacate the building; many made their exits through the windows. Some observers thought this riotous celebration portended a disaster for the nation; others regarded it as a sign that America had finally achieved democracy.

Jackson handled the presidency as he had handled everything else in his life—by taking firm control and brooking no interference. Although he sought advice, he acted according to his own ideas of right and wrong. His first task was to assemble his cabinet, which he did with an eye to recognizing the rising power of the western and central states as well the various interests within the Democratic party. For secretary of state he chose his political "magician," Martin Van Buren; his secretary of war was an old and loyal friend from Tennessee named John Eaton. His vice-president was Calhoun, who, at this point, still had Jackson's trust and respect.

"The reign of King Mob": Jackson's legendary inauguration-day celebration. Conservatives were horrified by the thousands of boisterous revelers on the presidential lawn, but the new president's grass-roots supporters were delighted. This, exulted one, was "a proud day for the people—General Jackson is *their own* president!"

It is to be regretted that the rich and powerful too often bend the acts of government to their selfish purposes.
—ANDREW JACKSON

As well as his official cabinet, Jackson also had a group of informal advisers known as the "kitchen cabinet." These were trusted political associates who had worked hard for his election. Among them were Francis P. Blair, editor of the Washington *Globe*, a staunchly pro-Jackson newspaper; Amos Kendall, another newspaper editor, who received an appointment as an auditor of the U.S. Treasury; and Roger B. Taney, who later became chief justice of the Supreme Court. Although his advisers had an important role in running the government, Jackson made up his own mind on most issues and often ignored their advice.

True to his inauguration-day promise, Old Hickory took a direct hand in changing the way the government was administered by introducing the concept of "rotation of office" to the federal government. In reality, this meant replacing supporters of Adams and Clay with Jackson loyalists. This practice was—and still is—known as the "spoils system," from the expression, "to the victor belong the spoils [prizes]."

Although Jackson did make many appointments, the number of people he removed from office was greatly exaggerated by his political enemies. During his eight years as president, he removed only 252 out of 612 high-level appointees, and about 900 of the 10,000 civil service employees. Not even all his avowed political enemies lost their jobs. The postmaster of Albany, New York, for example, was a veteran of the American Revolution but also an outspoken critic of the Jackson administration. Removed from office by Van Buren, the angry and bitter ex-postmaster confronted Jackson at a dinner party. "Sir," the old man said, as he began unbuttoning his jacket, "I have been removed as postmaster from Albany but there is something I wish to show you. I want you to see my wounds, sir, received while defending my country from the British . . . and my thanks is removal from my office, the only position I have to sustain me in my old age."

"Button your jacket," Jackson replied. "You are still postmaster."

An early 19th-century steam train. The first of the many U.S. railroads that would greatly aid and accelerate the nation's westward expansion was built in 1826. Unlike Henry Clay and the National Republicans, the Jacksonian Democrats favored the use of state rather than federal funds to develop roads, canals, and railroads.

Washington editor and presidential adviser Francis P. Blair (1791–1876). Except for Secretary of State Martin Van Buren (1782–1862), who was Jackson's close confidant, the president virtually ignored his offical cabinet. When he wanted advice, he talked to Blair and other members of the circle of political friends known as the "kitchen cabinet."

Jackson's personal loyalties sometimes caused him great embarrassment, however. Such was the result of the so-called "Eaton Affair," when Jackson's friend John N. Eaton, the senator from Tennessee, married Peggy O'Neale, the pretty and flirtatious daughter of a Washington innkeeper. In many ways the scandal was similar to the one over Jackson's own marriage. Peggy O'Neale had been married to a navy purser, who had died at sea. Gossips claimed the purser had committed suicide because of Eaton's attentions to his wife. The rumors flew even faster when Eaton proceeded to marry Peggy soon after her husband's death. Jackson's subsequent appointment of Eaton to be his secretary of war only served to aggravate an already difficult situation.

Unfortunately for Jackson, the wives of the other cabinet officers wanted no part of the new Mrs. Eaton. Led by Floride Calhoun, wife of the vice-president, the women of Washington ostracized her, shutting her out of their activities and generally making life miserable for her husband. Because Mrs. Eaton's troubles reminded him of the pain his wife had suffered from the tongues of gossips, Jackson gallantly defended the shunned woman, but Washington society still refused to accept her.

Actually, the affair probably had deeper roots than the question of Peggy O'Neale's morality. Calhoun coveted the presidency and assumed he would suc-

The destruction of our state governments or the annihilation of their control over the local concerns of the people would lead directly to revolution and anarchy, and finally to despotism and military domination.
—ANDREW JACKSON

Duff Green (1791–1875), editor of the *United States Telegraph*, a strongly pro-Jackson newspaper, was an early member of Jackson's "kitchen cabinet," but by 1830, his sympathies had begun to incline toward Vice-President John C. Calhoun. A year later, Green and his publication were openly aligned with Jackson's political enemies.

ceed Jackson. When Van Buren, who was Jackson's close friend and confidant, was appointed secretary of state, he became Calhoun's rival. In order to get rid of Van Buren, Calhoun embarked upon a scheme to drive Eaton out of the cabinet. Eaton's resignation, thought Calhoun, would trigger the resignation of the rest of the cabinet members and the formation of a new cabinet—without Van Buren.

The plan backfired on Calhoun when a crisis over states' rights surfaced after Congress passed legislation authorizing the imposition of high tariffs in 1828. Tariffs—taxes on imported goods—were wanted by New England manufacturers but were resented by southern and western farmers, who had to pay higher prices for their goods because of them. The Tariff of 1828 was particularly resented in Calhoun's home state of South Carolina, which officially adopted a paper, written by Calhoun, which argued that states had the right to "nullify" federal laws that went against their interests. The "nullification" issue, as it was known, created an uproar in Washington. The controversy came to a head on April 13, 1830, at a dinner honoring the birthday of Thomas Jefferson. After dinner, as was the custom, various dignitaries were called upon to deliver toasts. Jackson, prompted by Van Buren, raised his glass and directly challenged Calhoun with: "Our federal Union: it must be preserved!" Accepting the challenge, Calhoun responded: "The Union—next to our liberty the most dear."

Calhoun compounded his differences with Jackson by then publicizing yet another disagreement with the president, this one concerning Jackson's 1817 invasion of Florida. Jackson had always believed that Calhoun, then secretary of war, had defended his much-criticized actions in Florida. Now, receiving evidence that Calhoun had actually tried to have him punished for his conduct, the enraged Jackson asked his vice-president for an explanation of his earlier disloyalty. The matter might still have ended quietly and quickly had Calhoun not published some of the documents concerning the issue in a local newspaper, thereby making the controversy public. Jackson could not forgive this, and he resolved to force Calhoun from office.

The Eaton Affair gave Jackson his opportunity. After Van Buren and the other cabinet ministers resigned—just as Calhoun had planned—Jackson announced that he wanted Van Buren for his running mate when he ran for reelection in 1832. Calhoun realized his presidential chances were ruined; a year later, he resigned the vice-presidency and became senator from South Carolina. Van Buren was appointed by Jackson to be minister to England; Eaton became governor of Florida and then minister to Spain.

Illustrating the changes that Jackson made to the composition of his cabinet in 1830, a contemporary cartoon shows the president as an angry housekeeper emptying her kitchen of unwanted company. It was during this period that Vice-President Calhoun's plan to depose Secretary of State Van Buren by engineering the cabinet's mass resignation misfired, leaving Van Buren even more powerful than he had been before.

Washington socialite Peggy O'Neale (1799–1879), whose 1829 marriage to John Eaton (1790–1856), Jackson's good friend and secretary of war, precipitated a political crisis. Most Washingtonians believed that O'Neale had been involved with Eaton while her first husband was still alive. Jackson ignored his critics' charges that, by maintaining his association with Eaton, he was condoning "immorality."

The controversy with Calhoun reflected the major crisis that was brewing in the United States at this time. The issue concerned was that of states' rights versus the rights of the central government. This issue—under fierce debate to this day—was to be a major cause of the Civil War, which was fought some three decades later.

Although Jackson was a westerner with firm sympathies toward the South, particularly over the issue of slavery, he was becoming an increasingly strong advocate of strong central government. He was an ardent nationalist and vigorously opposed anything he perceived as a threat to the Union. For example, he vetoed the Maysville Bill of 1830, which would have provided federal funds for a section of the National Road, the nation's first superhighway, from Maysville, Kentucky, to Lexington, Kentucky. Jackson's veto of the Maysville Bill—one of 12 that he cast during his two administrations (far more than all his predecessors combined)—actually attacked several targets. One was internal improvements; another was Clay, who was a staunch advocate of internal improvements, particularly those within his home state of Kentucky; a third was Clay's newly emerging political party, the National Republicans.

In 1832 Jackson found himself—for once—on the same side of the political fence as Clay. Hoping to soothe the anger still simmering in the South over the Tariff of 1828, Clay introduced, and Jackson signed, a new tariff bill which, they believed, offered a compromise that would be found acceptable by all concerned. The Tariff of 1832 did lower some of the duties imposed by the 1828 legislation, but it retained duties on some of the items essential to southern planters, such as wool, iron, and hemp, which was used in making rope. As a result, South Carolina, led by Calhoun, declared the tariff "null and void," and threatened to secede from the Union should force be used to collect duties in the state.

Unofficially, Jackson threatened to hang Calhoun. Officially, he responded with both a carrot and a stick. He moved soldiers and supplies to South Carolina, and, in a proclamation addressed directly to the people of that state, he both praised them and warned them. "Disunion by armed force is *treason*," he said. "Are you ready to incur its guilt?" At the same time a "Force Bill" was introduced in Congress, which gave Jackson authority to use the U.S. Army and the U.S. Navy to collect customs duties.

The crisis was finally ended by a combination of events. Jackson urged Congress to be conciliatory and Clay—"the Great Pacificator"—introduced a compromise tariff, which Calhoun and the rest of the South accepted. Jackson signed both it and the "Force Bill" on the same day, just as his first term ended. A week later South Carolina repealed its tariff nullification act, but then, in a token gesture of bravado, it "nullified" the no longer necessary

Secretary of War John Eaton had been Jackson's friend and political supporter for many years before his marriage to Peggy O'Neale in 1829. When Jackson's advisers urged him to remove Eaton from the cabinet on the grounds that Eaton's relationship with O'Neale was immoral, the old warrior exploded. "I would resign the presidency," Jackson roared, "sooner than desert my friend Eaton."

"Force Bill." Through a display of tact and masterful politics, Jackson had prevented civil war—at least for the time being—and had further strengthened the concept of a strong central government.

The other major issue of Jackson's first term as president concerned Indian resettlement. The southern states were determined to be rid of their Indian populations in order to take possession of their land, and Jackson's response to the situation seemed almost to contradict his belief in a strong central government or at least to prove that he did not always oppose states' rights.

The Indians, primarily the Cherokees, Creeks, Choctaws, and Chickasaws, did not want to leave their ancestral lands, and they turned to the central government for protection. At the heart of the crisis was a compact made in 1802 between the federal government and the state of Georgia; the United

Washington's gossips and cartoonists had a field day when Jackson took the unusual step of assembling his cabinet to consider the alleged "immorality" of Secretary of War John Eaton's bride, Peggy O'Neale. In this version of the meeting, Mrs. Eaton, dressed here as a dancing girl, points her toe as Jackson pronounces her a "charming creature."

Choctaw Indians playing lacrosse, a game that white men adopted in the 1830s. However, when American Indians began to adopt white men's practices—including government under a written constitution—many settlers feared that the "civilized" red men would become even more difficult to dislodge from their ancestral lands.

States had agreed to remove the Indians from Georgia at some future date in return for Georgia's ceding its western lands to the federal government. Since the government had been slow in fulfilling its side of the bargain, Georgia began seizing Creek and Cherokee lands on its own authority during the 1820s. The Indians, aided by eastern humanitarians and church groups, appealed to the Supreme Court, where they won two major decisions, handed down by Chief Justice John Marshall. These victories, however, were hollow because the govern-

Torn from the Georgia land where they had lived for centuries, Cherokee Indians make their painful journey west in 1838. Of this forced exodus (which is now known to history as "The Trail of Tears"), poet and essayist Ralph Waldo Emerson (1803–1882) wrote: "Such a denial of justice, and such deafness to screams for mercy were never heard . . . since the earth was made."

ment did nothing to enforce the decisions. Jackson, after one landmark decision, *Worcester* vs. *Georgia* (1832), is supposed to have said: "Well, John Marshall has made his decision, now let him enforce it."

In 1830 Congress had passed the Indian Removal Act, which seemed to offer a reasonable solution to the stalemate. Under the act, it was proposed that the Indians should cede their lands within the states to the federal government in exchange for new homes in the unsettled territories west of the Mississippi River. The act authorized the president to protect the Indians in their new tribal areas, to pay them for improvements they had made on their old land, and to subsidize both their move and their first year's expenses in the West.

Under the best of conditions, the removal program would not have been a proud chapter in American history, but what occurred was deplorable. While some of the tribes submitted, packing their belongings and heading for the barren land the government had offered them, many other Indians—notably the Cherokees in Georgia—refused to move. Finally, in 1838 (after Jackson had left office) Georgia militiamen brutally rounded up more than 17,000 Cherokees. The helpless Indians were forced to travel, by steamboat, crowded boxcar, and by foot, to Arkansas, 800 miles from their homes. Four thousand of the once proud and strong Cherokees died of disease, starvation, and exposure during the forced march, now known to history as "The Trail of Tears."

For his part in the events that led up to this disgraceful episode, Jackson is often remembered as an Indian hater, but the truth is more complicated.

As president, he responded to what America's citizens wanted: the removal of the Indians. He also believed that the Indians were the government's responsibility. Jackson knew that if the tribes had remained in place they would have been annihilated by land-hungry white settlers. As an old Indian fighter, Jackson was not the benevolent protector of the Native Americans, but neither was he their sworn enemy.

In fact, Jackson had adopted a Creek Indian baby he found abandoned after a battle in 1813. The boy, whom Jackson named Lyncoyer, was raised at the Hermitage, where he was educated and well cared for until he died of tuberculosis at age 17.

Jackson believed that the Indian Removal program offered an honorable solution to a difficult problem. As conceived, the program promised to give the southern tribes a new home with a chance to have their own state and better protection from encroaching whites. That the promise was not fulfilled was not solely Jackson's fault.

A portrait of Jackson by Thomas Sully (1783–1872). Although Sully, whose subjects had included many prominent American political figures, was one of the 19th century's leading artists, his likeness of Jackson was considered unsuccessful. Many felt that it failed to capture the strong spirit and tough-mindedness that characterized "Old Hickory."

OF VETO MEMORY.

HAD I BEEN CONSULTED.

KING ANDREW THE FIRST.

7

King Andrew I

The major issue of Jackson's second administration was his war with the Bank of the United States. The roots of this war went back to his early life, when, like many other frontier citizens, he had engaged in land speculation, buying and selling thousands of acres. During that period, investing in land was the quickest way to make money in the West. Much of this business was conducted by exchanges of paper—promissory notes guaranteeing future payment for purchases in hard (gold and silver) currency. Jackson lost a great deal of money when a series of promissory notes he had accepted turned out to be worthless; the experience left him with a deep and permanent distrust of paper currency. His dislike of "paper" and banks was strengthened by a major financial panic: in 1819 many of the nation's banks, which had issued more paper currency than they could back with gold, collapsed, resulting in financial ruin for thousands of people.

Jackson's dispute with the Bank of the United States was based, not on economics, but on politics. The bank, or BUS, as it was known, was a private corporation with a charter from the federal government, which owned one-fifth of its stock. The BUS

"King Andrew the First," an 1832 anti-Jackson campaign poster. Jackson, accused by the National Republican party of exceeding his authority, is shown clutching a ruler's scepter in one hand and a veto in the other as he tramples on the U.S. Constitution and the Bank of the United States.

President of the Bank of the United States Nicholas Biddle (1786–1844), who created a financial crisis in 1832 by calling in loans as part of his attempt to counter Jackson's attack upon the BUS, as the bank was known.

also had the exclusive right to hold the government's money. Based in Philadelphia, and with branches in 29 other cities, the BUS did an enormous amount of general banking business. It was important to the economic welfare of the country because of the credit it supplied to business and industry; because its banknotes, which circulated nationwide, were a dependable medium of exchange at a time when there was no standard money in the United States; and because it prevented state and local banks from issuing more paper money than they had gold to back. (The BUS, chartered for 20 years in 1816, had been little more successful in living up to the government's expectations than had its predecessor, the First Bank of the United States, which went out of business in 1811.)

The president of the Bank of the United States was a cautious and able Philadelphia aristocrat named Nicholas Biddle. Because he personally owned much of the bank's stock, Biddle had the power to appoint all the bank's officials, to decide who would get credit, to set interest rates, and to control the supply of currency in the country by issuing paper money that could be redeemed for gold or silver.

Like other "hard money" men, Jackson believed that gold and silver were the only "safe" forms of money. Advocates of hard money condemned all "folding" money, whether it was issued by state banks or by the Bank of the United States. Jackson was convinced that the BUS was detrimental to the interests of the American people because its virtual control of the nation's economy threatened to make it even more powerful than the federal government. He wanted a bank in which the government could deposit funds, but he wanted it established under the supervision of the U.S. Treasury Department, with its officials appointed by the U.S. president. Accordingly, as soon as he became president, Jackson began to seek ways to limit the bank's power. In his first annual message to Congress in 1829, Jackson raised doubts about rechartering the bank, and in other statements he promised to "chain the monster," as he called the bank.

Biddle, whom the Jacksonians called "Tsar Nicholas," was sophisticated, proud, and not easily intimidated. One of the most powerful men in the United States, he often referred to Jackson in terms of contempt. "This worthy President," he once sneered, "thinks that because he has scalped Indians and imprisoned Judges, he is to have his way with the Bank. He is mistaken." (During the Battle of New Orleans, Jackson had arrested a federal judge who had released a prisoner Jackson considered dangerous.)

Biddle was keenly aware of the danger posed to the BUS by Jackson's hostility. Although the bank's charter, which gave it the right to function, was not due to be renewed until 1836, Biddle, acting on the advice of a small number of government officials who, as events would prove, had overestimated popular support for the bank, decided to ask Congress to recharter the bank four years early, in 1832. Biddle and his friends in the administration were calculating that, since 1832 was an election year and Jackson was running for reelection, the president would not wish to do anything that might alienate

A cartoon illustrates the American public's impatience with Jackson's war against the Bank of the United States. A friend—representing the president's supporters—tries to haul Jackson back to reality, but the dreaming president continues to battle a "monster"—Jackson's own word for the bank.

the bank's powerful friends in Congress. The rechartering bill passed both houses of Congress with little difficulty. All that remained was for Jackson to sign it into law.

A cartoon entitled "The Downfall of Mother Bank" shows a triumphant Jackson watching as Nicholas Biddle and his fellow "varmints" flee from the crashing pillars of the Bank of the United States. The scroll in Jackson's hand reads: "Order for the removal of the public money deposited in the United States Bank."

You are a den of vipers and thieves. I intend to rout you out, and by the eternal God, I will rout you out.
—ANDREW JACKSON
speaking to a delegation of bankers who supported the Bank of the United States

When the bill came to the President's House for his signature, Jackson was temporarily bedridden; his health, weakened by the mental and physical wounds he had suffered over the years, had dete-

A snuffbox decorated with portraits of Jackson (top) and other political leaders is typical of the items that began to proliferate in election campaigns during the 1820s. From that point on, no American election has been without a deluge of souvenirs, hats, pins, banners, costumes, posters, slogans, and other mementoes.

riorated under the burdens of the presidency. As he was reading the bill, Van Buren stopped by for a visit and was shocked at Jackson's haggard appearance. Upon seeing his good friend, however, Old Hickory brightened. "The bank, Mr. Van Buren," he rasped, "is trying to kill me, *but I will kill it!*"

As good as his word, Jackson vetoed the rechartering bill. His July 10, 1832, veto message to Congress demonstrated his masterful political skills. He called the bank a dangerous monopoly whose profits came "out of the earnings of the American people," and he asserted that its stock was held only by members "of the richest class" and by foreigners who could use their holdings in the bank to influence America's affairs. He refused, he said, to permit the "prostitution of our Government to the advancement of the few at the expense of the many." The government, he declared, should give "equal protection and equal benefits" to all Americans.

The veto message, with its stirring, nationalistic tone, strongly appealed to the American working man. Biddle dismissed it as a "manifesto of anarchy," but the bank's supporters in Congress were unable to override the veto. Even fiery speeches by Henry Clay, the most eloquent man in Congress and a firm supporter of the bank, failed to have any impact on Jackson's decision.

The BUS controversy then became the major issue of the 1832 election, which pitted National Republican Clay against Democrat Jackson. However, the Democrats' landslide victory was probably due less to the voters' dislike of the bank, or of Clay, than to their immense affection for Jackson. "My opinion," said a defeated National Republican candidate, "is that he may be president for life if he chooses."

Now Old Hickory could continue his war against the bank with a vengeance. "I have it chained," he boasted, "*the monster must perish.*" Instead of waiting for the bank's inevitable demise when its charter expired in 1836, Jackson withdrew the government's money from the BUS and deposited it in selected state banks (Jackson's enemies called them "pet" banks). Biddle countered this move by calling in loans, hoping that the resulting public distress would force Jackson to extend the bank's charter. Neither the near panic created by this move, nor other tactics, such as persuading Congress to censure Jackson for his war against the bank, deterred Old Hickory; and, in the end, he won. The BUS charter expired in 1836, and Jackson remained as popular with the people as ever. Biddle's bank, by then chartered as a state institution, failed in 1841; the defeated Philadelphian retired to his country estate, where he died three years later at the age of 58.

One result of the bank war was the creation of a new political party in the United States consisting of National Republicans, some Democrats, a number of "nullifiers" (advocates of states' rights), and bankers. They called themselves "Whigs," after the party in England that stood for limiting the powers of the monarch. The Whigs asserted that the United States now had its own monarch, whom they mockingly called "King Andrew I" because of what they considered his high-handed and tyrannical actions.

His enemies could call him what they wished. Old Hickory did not care. He did what he considered

As Jackson (third from left) stares in disbelief, a gunman levels a pistol at him on January 30, 1835. The assailant, a deranged house painter named Richard Lawrence, carried two pistols, but both misfired and Jackson was unhurt. Jackson was the first U.S. president to be the target of an assassination attempt.

The Alamo, a San Antonio, Texas, fort defended by 184 Texans, fell to a 3,000-man force led by Mexican General Antonio López de Santa Anna (1794–1876) on March 6, 1836. Every Texan, including legendary frontiersman Davy Crockett (1786–1836), was killed in the battle—or brutally gunned down after it. "Remember the Alamo!" became the war cry of Texas.

right, and most of the people in America not only supported him, they worshiped him. Under Jackson's administration, the United States, for the only time in its history, had no national debt, thanks to the huge sums of money pouring into the federal treasury from tariffs and the sale of public lands to settlers. So much land was being sold and so much speculation was occurring, however, that Jackson decided that it was time to put into action his plan for making hard money the only currency acceptable for business transactions involving the federal government. On July 11, 1836, he issued his Specie Circular, which declared that only hard money could be used to pay for federal land. This well-intentioned measure ended the wild speculation in public land, but it also produced the panic of 1837, in which hundreds of banks and businesses failed and unemployment swept the nation. The ensuing depression was the worst the country had ever experienced, but since it occurred after Jackson left office, it did not diminish his popularity with the people.

Jackson dealt with foreign affairs just as he did with domestic issues. To accomplish his goals,

Jackson combined patience and tact with the threat of force. This approach led to some striking successes. He worked out an agreement with Great Britain concerning trade in the West Indies, and he solved a nagging difficulty with the French over claims for property damages during the wars between Britain and France, which had ended in 1815. Jackson also met with several failures in the area of foreign policy. One concerned the boundary dispute betwen Maine and Canada, which had remained unresolved since the American Revolution and which was not settled until the Webster-Ashburton Treaty of 1842.

A more notable failure was Jackson's attempt to buy Texas from Mexico, a transaction the Mexicans refused even to consider. Meanwhile, Americans were flooding into Texas. The result was a revolution that the Texans won. When Texas declared independence in 1836, it appealed to the United States either to recognize its independence or to annex it. Although he was an ardent nationalist and anxious to add Texas to the Union, Jackson hesitated because he feared Mexico would declare war on the United States. Furthermore, his protégé Martin Van Buren was a candidate for president in 1836 and Jackson wanted to do nothing that would jeopardize his chances. Jackson also realized that the annexation of Texas would spark a crisis in Congress over the expansion of slavery, an issue that was soon to tear the United States apart. Thus, as usual, Jackson waited patiently for the right moment before acting. He did nothing until his last full day in office—March 3, 1837—and then, with congressional approval, he officially recognized the independence of Texas.

> *Except an enormous fabric of Executive power, the President has built up nothing. . . . He goes for destruction, universal destruction.*
> —HENRY CLAY
> leading opponent of Jackson

Texans celebrate the birth of the Lone Star Republic in 1836, a year before its recognition by the United States. Jackson made no effort to stop the hundreds of American citizens who illegally joined the Texas army, but he maintained diplomatic silence about recognizing the new nation until the day before he left office.

8

"I Am Dying as Fast as I Can"

Although inauguration day, 1837, was officially a celebration to welcome the new president, Martin Van Buren, it was really a tribute to Andrew Jackson. Senator Thomas Hart Benton of Missouri, once Old Hickory's enemy and now his staunch friend, probably put it best when he said: "For once, the rising was eclipsed by the setting sun."

Van Buren's election to the presidency in 1836 had greatly pleased Jackson, who viewed it as a popular endorsement of his actions as president. Indeed, some people suggested that the election should have been recorded as Old Hickory's third presidential victory because the voters had merely reaffirmed their trust in him by electing Van Buren.

In his farewell message to the nation, issued on inauguration day, Jackson noted the victories his administration had won in its battles with special-interest groups; he warned the American people about the increasing danger of sectionalism, which threatened to divide the country; and he spoke warmly about the importance of the federal Union. As for himself, he said: "My own race is nearly run;

Martin Van Buren, Jackson's vice-president and successor, was a shrewd politician and an able and intelligent chief executive. His popularity, however, was undermined by the 1837 financial panic, for which the Whigs branded him "Martin Van Ruin." He was swept out of office after one term.

Shortly before his death, Jackson posed for this portrait by Mathew Brady (c. 1823–1896), later famed for his Civil War photographs. Jackson, weak and ill at 78, still carefully shaved himself and brushed his hair, which, noted a friend, "continues to add to the dignity of his appearance."

advanced age and failing health warn me that before long I must pass beyond the reach of human events and cease to feel the vicissitudes of human affairs. . . . I bid you a last and affectionate farewell."

Three days later, Jackson began his final trip home. Now worn and feeble, just a few days short of his 70th birthday, he stopped frequently, resting as he visited friends and received the accolades of an adoring public. Cheering crowds blocked his path everywhere along the route to Nashville, which he finally reached several weeks later.

Unfortunately, his homecoming was not all it could have been. While he had been in Washington, the plantation had been managed by Andrew Jackson, Jr., who had been adopted by Jackson and his wife in 1809. Young Jackson had proved to be a careless manager, and his father found the Hermitage badly neglected and burdened with debts. Thanks to the intercession of some of his old and

Most visitors to the Hermitage were impressed by its understated elegance. "The first thing that struck me," said a Frenchman who called on Jackson, "was the simplicity of his house. I asked myself if this could really be the dwelling of the most popular man in the United States."

The drawing room of the Hermitage, now a public museum. After a fire partially destroyed the mansion in 1831, Jackson had the building refurbished and enlarged. Architects who restored the house in 1974 were surprised by the high quality of the materials and workmanship Jackson had employed.

trusted friends, however, Jackson was able to repair the estate and repay the debts.

The improved condition of Jackson's affairs stood in great contrast to the state into which the country had fallen. Van Buren was unable to resolve the nationwide economic crisis that resulted from Jackson's Specie Circular. In 1840 Van Buren lost his bid for a second term to the Whig candidate, William Henry Harrison. Van Buren's defeat greatly saddened Jackson, who now said he hoped to live long enough to see the Democrats returned to power. He did not have long to wait; Harrison died of pneumonia within a month of his inauguration, and the

A cartoon satirizes conditions during the financial panic that swept the U.S. in 1837. As workmen (right) stand idly with their tools, depositors (center) try to redeem their worthless bank notes, and a crowd gathers at the pawnshop of "Shylock Graspall," located next to the liquor store, whose patrons (left) drown their sorrows.

presidency passed to his vice-president, John Tyler, a former Democrat whose policies reassured Jackson. One of the most important policies pursued by the new president was the annexation of Texas, which Tyler recommended to Congress just as his term of office was about to expire. "All is safe at last!" exclaimed Jackson, an ardent nationalist to the end.

Politics was one of the few pleasures remaining to the old warrior, whose physical condition had deteriorated rapidly in the years since his departure from the President's House. He was in constant pain and coughed incessantly. Tuberculosis was consuming his lungs, and dropsy was causing his body to swell. But no matter how ill he might be, he eagerly read the newspapers and the many letters he received daily. The letters from Washington he opened first.

He also welcomed the steady stream of well-wishers and office seekers who continually besieged him. "I am dying as fast as I can," he remarked with wry humor, "and they all know it, but they will keep swarming upon me in crowds, intriguing for office."

Despite the best medical care available, Jackson's physical condition steadily worsened. He had constant, shattering headaches, and toward the end, unable to lie down comfortably, he spent his time propped up with pillows in his favorite chair. Still, he continued to answer the many letters he received and to entertain his visitors.

Finally, on June 2, 1845, desperate to relieve the old man's pain, his family summoned a doctor from Nashville. The doctor managed to drain some of the fluid that was causing his body to swell, but the treatment left Jackson even weaker than before. Six days later, the family again called the doctor, who saw that Old Hickory was now very close to death. Jackson fainted as he was moved from his chair to his bed. When he awoke, he saw that the room was filled with family, friends, and servants; many of them were weeping. "My dear children, and friends and servants," he whispered, "I hope and trust to meet you all in heaven, both white and black." A little later, so that he could see his visitors better,

The master of the Hermitage in retirement. Jackson's intellect and style were unimpaired in his final years. He spent his days inspecting his plantation, and his evenings conducting family prayers and reading and discussing politics, which never lost their fascination for him.

Jackson asked for his spectacles. When he spoke of his coming death, many of them began crying again. "What is the matter with my dear children?" he asked. "Have I alarmed you? Oh, do not cry. Be good children, and we will all meet in heaven." These were his last words. Later that same day—June 8, 1845—Andrew Jackson died, at the age of 78.

Shortly after Jackson's death, Sam Houston, the first governor of Texas and an old friend with whom Jackson had soldiered during the War of 1812, arrived at the Hermitage with his young son. When he saw that he was too late to say farewell to his old comrade in arms, the tough, battle-scarred Houston

Surrounded by family and friends, Andrew Jackson died, at age 78, on June 8, 1845. Racked with the pain of old wounds and disease, Jackson remained resolute and without self-pity to the end. "I am in the hands of the Lord, who is about to relieve me," he told his grieving family. "You should rejoice, not weep!"

A commemorative engraving published soon after Jackson's death. Jackson's burial service was a scene of uninhibited grief, with blacks and whites sharing their sorrow. One of those present said: "Death did not make all equal more completely than did this funeral."

Faults he had, undoubtedly; such faults as often belong to an ardent, generous, sincere nature—the weeds that grow in rich soil. Notwithstanding this, he was precisely the man for the period in which he fell and nobly discharged the duties demanded of him by the times.
—WILLIAM CULLEN BRYANT
American poet and editor,
writing in December 1836

fell to his knees by Jackson's open coffin and began to cry. "My son," Houston said, turning to the boy, "try to remember that you have looked upon the face of Andrew Jackson."

After an emotional funeral service attended by a throng of mourners, Jackson was buried at the Hermitage, next to his beloved Rachel.

Jackson's old friend, General Sam Houston (1793–1863), became the national hero of independent Texas when he defeated the armies of Mexico in 1836. A politician, soldier, landowner, and diplomat, Houston was twice elected president of the Republic of Texas.

9

The Legacy of Andrew Jackson

Among historians, who often disagree in their opinions of leaders and their policies, there is little consensus with regard to Andrew Jackson. Some scholars have referred to Jackson himself as an "unmitigated disaster for the nation" and to his administration as "deplorable." Others, praising his "confidence and imagination," his "pugnacity," and his "capacity for quick but correct decisions," rank him with such presidents as George Washington, Thomas Jefferson, Abraham Lincoln, and Franklin D. Roosevelt. Few would deny, however, that Jackson, a product of the frontier, unpolished and poorly educated, expanded the powers of the American presidency and firmly established "Jacksonian democracy"—"the American doctrine," as Franklin D. Roosevelt described it, "that dedicates itself to the end that the American people shall . . . remain the custodians of their own destiny."

Indeed, Old Hickory redefined the presidency. To avoid the dangers of a dictatorship or a monarchy, the men who wrote the Constitution divided the powers of the federal government among three

Andrew Jackson demonstrated that any American, rich or poor, has a chance to be great, and that every American has the right to help shape the nation's destiny. Jackson's heritage, said the 32nd U.S. president, Franklin D. Roosevelt (1882–1945), is "his unending contribution to the vitality of our democracy."

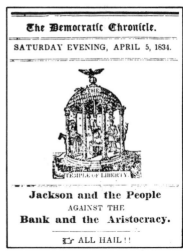

The Democratic Chronicle.

SATURDAY EVENING, APRIL 5, 1834.

TEMPLE OF LIBERTY.

Jackson and the People
AGAINST THE
Bank and the Aristocracy.

☞ ALL HAIL !!

The "Temple of Liberty," an early Democratic party symbol. Although today's Democrats consider Jefferson their party's founder, it was actually born during Jackson's 1828 election. Agreeing with Jefferson that government should represent the majority, Jackson nevertheless attacked Jefferson's "aristocratic" concepts, insisting that the "common man" could best fill government offices.

branches: the executive (the presidency); the legislative (the Congress); and the judiciary (the courts). Each branch was designed to prevent either of the others from gaining absolute and unchecked power. Although Jackson's predecessors accepted the concept of three separate but equal parts, he did not. Jackson electrified his contemporaries by announcing that "the president is the direct representative of the American people." This concept is taken for granted today, but it was considered radical at the time. Jackson insisted that it was the president's responsibility to establish national policy, to manage public affairs, and to present legislation to Congress on behalf of the people. Following Jackson's redefinition of presidential executive power and responsibility, he and all his successors were indisputably the heads of the United States government.

Old Hickory also discovered the value of the president's veto power, which enabled him to "kill" unfavorable legislation. Furthermore, he was the first president to use the "pocket veto." This is the means whereby a president can cancel legislation by simply not signing a bill after Congress has adjourned. (If Congress is still in session a bill automatically becomes law 10 days after it is passed unless the president does veto it. However, many bills are not passed until the end of the congressional year, and the president can then "pocket" them.)

Jackson's impact on the political life of the United States was also significant. Because of his forceful personality, two strong political parties emerged and the American people, many of whom had only recently gained the right to vote, became intensely interested in politics.

The rise of democracy—government by the people—and the decline of privilege were also part of Jackson's legacy. The Age of Jackson, as scholars have come to call the era between the War of 1812 and the Civil War, saw the rise of the "common man" and marked the emergence of a new breed of politician. After Jackson, no American politician could afford not to support the gospel of popular rule. Democracy was now becoming a reality as well as a

concept. By his own example, Jackson demonstrated that any American male could be elected to high public office and be capable of managing the administration of his country. Jackson, notes historian Robert V. Remini, "was the nation's image of itself." Admittedly, a country that permitted slavery, denied citizenship to Indians, and permitted women neither to own property nor to vote had not yet achieved true and full democracy. Nevertheless, the Jacksonian era marked new directions in the administration of government and heralded the emergence of modern American political life.

For the United States, the 19th century was not only a period of profound political and economic change, it was an era of enormous geographical expansion. More than two-thirds of the land within the country's present borders was acquired between 1803 and 1900.

A steamboat on New York City's East River in 1837. America's economy, like its political scene, was transformed forever during the half-century known as the Age of Jackson. New methods of manufacturing and transportation were rapidly converting the isolated agrarian nation of Jefferson's day into a highly industrialized world power.

Further Reading

Buell, Augustus C. *History of Andrew Jackson*. New York: Charles Scribner's Sons, 1904.

James, Marquis. *The Life of Andrew Jackson*. New York: The Bobbs-Merrill Company, 1938.

Remini, Robert V. *Andrew Jackson and the Course of American Empire, 1767–1821, Vol. 1*. New York: Harper & Row Publishers, Inc., 1977.

———. *Andrew Jackson and the Course of American Freedom, 1822–1832, Vol. 2*. New York: Harper & Row Publishers, Inc., 1981.

———. *Andrew Jackson and the Course of American Democracy, 1833–1845, Vol. 3*. New York: Harper & Row Publishers, Inc., 1984.

Schlesinger, Arthur M., jr. *The Age of Jackson*. Boston, Massachusetts: Little, Brown & Company, 1945.

Ward, John William. *Andrew Jackson: Symbol for an Age*. New York: Oxford University Press, Inc., 1962.

Williams, T. Harry, Richard N. Current and Frank Freidel. *A History of the United States*. New York: Alfred A. Knopf, Inc., 1964.

Chronology

March 15, 1767	Born Andrew Jackson, in the Waxhaws region of the Carolinas
Sept. 26, 1787	Certified to practice law
Feb. 15, 1791	Appointed attorney general of Tennessee's Mero District
Jan. 18, 1794	Marries Rachel Donelson Robards for second time after their first marriage—held three years earlier—is determined to be invalid
1796	Elected Tennessee's first member of U.S. House of Representatives
1797	Elected to U.S. Senate by Tennessee legislature
1798	Resigns from Senate and is appointed judge of Superior Court of Tennessee
1802	Elected major general of Tennessee militia
1813	Leads Tennessee militiamen on arduous march home from Natchez, Mississippi, earning nickname "Old Hickory"
March 27, 1814	Defeats Creek Indians at Battle of Horseshoe Bend
	Appointed major general in charge of U.S. Army's Seventh Military District
Jan. 8, 1815	Defeats British at Battle of New Orleans
1817–18	Invades Florida in punitive operation against Seminole Indians and overthrows the territory's Spanish government
1824–25	Loses to John Quincy Adams in bid for presidency despite winning plurality of popular vote
Dec. 22, 1828	Rachel Jackson dies of a heart attack
March 4, 1829	Jackson becomes seventh president of the United States
1830	Signs Indian Removal Act, which calls for relocation of several tribes from southern states to unsettled areas west of the Mississippi River
1832	Elected to second term as president
1836–37	Jackson's Specie Circular, a measure requiring payment in hard currency for purchases of federal land, produces economic depression later known as panic of 1837
1837	Jackson retires to the Hermitage, his family home in Tennessee, as a private citizen
June 8, 1845	Dies, aged 78, at the Hermitage, of natural causes

Index

Jackson, Robert (Andrew Jackson's brother), 25–26
"Jacksonian democracy," 103
James, William, 8
Jay Treaty, 30
Jefferson, Thomas, 39–40, 51, 72, 103, 107
Kendall, Amos, 68
Key, Francis Scott, 49
Lawrence, James, 14
Lawrence, Richard, 89
Lenin, Vladimir, 8
Lewis, Meriwether, 41
Lincoln, Abraham, 11, 103
McCay, Spruce, 26
Madison, James, 40
Marshall, John, 65–66, 77, 80
Marxism, 7, 8
Maysville Bill of 1830, 74
Miami, Florida, 8
Mobile, Alabama, 16
Monroe, James, 52–53
Munich, 8
Nashville, Tennessee, 27, 29–30, 94, 98
    see also Tennessee
Natchez, Mississippi, 41, 47
National Republican party, 69, 75, 88
National Road, 75
New Orleans, Battle of, 13–21, 40–41, 51, 85
New York City, 8, 107
Niebuhr, Reinhold, 10
"Old Ironsides" see USS Constitution
O'Neale, Peggy, 70–71, 73–76
Pakenham, Sir Edward, 14, 19–20
panic of 1837, 90, 96
Pensacola, Florida, 53
Red Eagle (leader of the Creek Indians) see Weatherford, William
Remini, Robert V., 105
Roane, Archibald, 37
Robards, Lewis, 29–30
Roosevelt, Franklin D., 8, 103
Sacajawea, 41
St. Marks, Florida, 53
Salisbury, North Carolina, 26–27

Santa Anna, Antonio López de, 90, 101
Seminole Indians, 52–53
Sevier, John, 37
Shawnee Indians, 50
slavery, 16, 74, 105
South Carolina, 57
    nullification of Tariff of 1832, 72–73, 75–76, 89
Specie Circular, 90, 95
"Star-Spangled Banner, The," 49
Stokes, John, 26
Sully, Thomas, 81
Taney, Roger B., 68
Tariff of 1828, 72, 75
Tariff of 1832, 75
Tecumseh, 50
Tennessee, 30, 37, 50, 55–56
    see also Nashville, Tennessee
Texas, 90–91, 98, 101
Tippecanoe, Battle of, 50
Tolstoy, Leo, 7
Tyler, John, 98
United States Telegraph, 71
USS Chesapeake, 14
USS Constitution, 42
Van Buren, Martin, 60, 67–68, 70, 72–73, 88, 91, 93, 95
War and Peace, 7
War of 1812, 40, 42, 52, 99, 104
    Battle of New Orleans, 13–21, 40–41, 51, 85
    causes of, 14–15
    Treaty of Ghent, 13–15, 51–52, 56–57
Washington, D.C., 63, 66
    burned by the British, 47–48
Washington, George, 15, 30, 53, 103
Washington Globe, 68
Waxhaws, 23–24
Weatherford, William, 52
Webster-Ashburton Treaty of 1842, 91
Whig party, 89, 93, 95
Wilkinson, James, 39–42
Wilson, Woodrow, 8
Worcester vs. Georgia, 80
Zangara, Giuseppe, 8

Herman J. Viola received his B.A. and M.A. from Marquette University and his Ph.D. from Indiana University. He has been assistant editor of the *Indiana Magazine of History* and the editor of *Prologue: The Journal of the National Archives,* which he founded in 1968. Since 1972, Dr. Viola has served as director of the National Anthropological Archives at the Smithsonian Institution. His major publications include *Thomas L. McKenney* (1974), *The Indian Legacy of Charles Bird King* (1976), *Diplomats in Buckskin* (1981), and the *National Archives of the United States.*

Arthur M. Schlesinger, jr., taught history at Harvard for many years and is currently Albert Schweitzer Professor of the Humanities at City University of New York. He is the author of numerous highly praised works in American history and has twice been awarded the Pulitzer Prize. He served in the White House as special assistant to presidents Kennedy and Johnson.